Good Dirt
The Complete Mountain Bike Guide to Sun Valley, Idaho

Published by

Go Right, LLC
Hailey, ID 83333

email: gmcbob@yahoo.com

All black and white photos by the author unless otherwise noted.

Other titles by Go Right LLC include:

> Good Dirt
> Good Dirt II
> Sun Spots - The Adventurous Travelers Guide to Sun Valley, Idaho
> A Weekend in Grandma's Underwear
> Have You Seen My Hair?
> How To Screw Your Neighbor In One Easy Lawsuit
> Happy Hiking 3

Cover design by Handis N. Mypants (Greg McRoberts)
Book layout, design and authored by Yur Nemesis (Greg McRoberts)
Maps by Where M. Eye (Greg McRoberts)

This book is dedicated to everyone in the Wood River and Sawtooth valleys who have contributed their efforts, both physically and financially, to the extensive trail systems we are able to enjoy. This would include the USFS, motorcyclists, private individuals, hikers, equestrians, mountain bikers, the BLM and countless others.

Thank you.

"The fool who knows he is a fool
is for that reason very wise.
The fool who thinks himself wise
is the greatest fool of all."

For Quinn

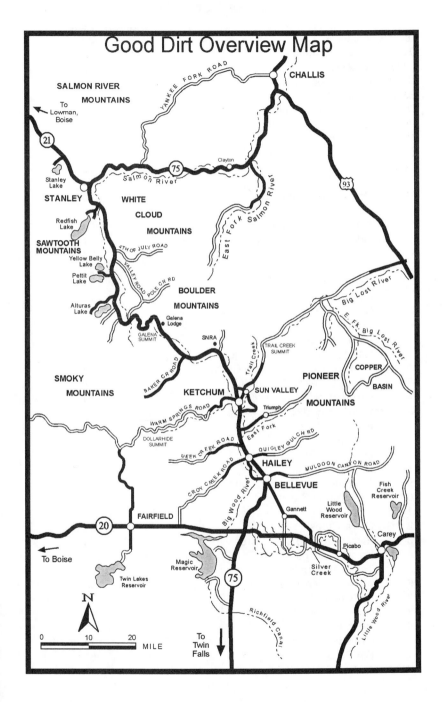

Good Dirt Overview Map

Table of Contents

You may be aware of some rides that are missing from this guidebook that were in the past two editions. Then again, you may not because it appears that no one ever rode them. Either way, they're gone.

The USFS asked that some of these rides be removed like Baker Lake, due to density-usage problems. Why compete with all those hikers and equestrians when there are SO many other awesome trails to ride? The other rides omitted from this third edition simply were not great mountain bike rides and thus, they never got used.

This book contains the best and most comprehensive selection of mountain bike rides in the Sawtooth and Wood River Valleys. Why waste expensive paper on the less than mediocre rides? Our thoughts exactly.

Best Easy Rides

Best Date Rides

Best Gonzo/Hard Rides

Best Night Rides

Our Favorite Good Dirt Rides

Local Bike Shops (Service & Rental)

Backwoods Mountain Sports - Warm Springs Rd & Main St, 726-8818
Durance Cycleworks - 131 2nd St - 726-7693
The Elephant's Perch - 280 East Ave - 726-3497
Formula Sports - 460 N Main - 726-3194
Kelly Sports - Colonnade Bldg Sun Valley Rd - 726-8503
Pete Lanes - Sun Valley Village - 622-2279
Pete Lanes - River Run Plaza at Bald Mountain - 622-6144
Ski Tek - 191 Sun Valley Rd - 726-7503
Sturtos - 380 N Main - 726-4512
Sturtevants in Hailey - 201 N Main - 788-7847
Sun Summit - 791 Warm Springs Rd - 726-0707
Sun Summit South in Hailey - 418 S Main - 788-6006

Local Coffee Scene

Hailey:
Hailey Coffee Company - 219 S Main
Java on Main - 310 N Main
Cucina Cafe - 620 N Main

Ketchum:
The Grinder - 4th & Leadville
Java on Fourth - 191 4th St
Starbucks - Main St & Sun Valley Rd
Tully's - 601 Sun Valley Rd

Motel/Hotel Info

Bellevue:
High Country Motel and Cabins - 788-2050
Come On Inn - 788-0825
Hailey:
Airport Inn - 788-2477
Wood River Inn - 578-0600
Ketchum:
Bald Mountain Lodge - 726-9963
Tyrolean Lodge - 726-5336
Clarion Inn - 726-5601
Kentwood Lodge - 726-4114
Ketchum Korral Motor Lodge - 726-3510
Lift Tower Lodge - 726-5163
Tamarack Lodge - 726-3344
Area Reservations:
Sun Valley Area Reservations - 726-3660
Base Mountain Properties - 726-5601
Classic Lodging - 727-6805
Sun Valley Lodge Reservations - 622-2151

General Information

Ketchum Ranger District	208-622-5371
Stanley Ranger District	208-774-3681
Sawtooth National Recreation Area	208-726-7672
Lost River Ranger District	208-588-2224
Yankee Fork Ranger District	208-838-2201
Emergency	**911**

Useful Local Area Web-sites:
Sawtooth National Recreation Area: www.fs.fed.us/r4/sawtooth/
Salmon-Challis National Forest: www.fs.fed.us/r4/sc/
United States Forest Service: www.fs.fed.us/
Sun Valley Guide On-Line: www.svguide.com/
Sun Valley Area Reservations: www.inidaho.com
Sun Valley Area Reservations: www.sun-valley-idaho.com
Sun Valley Resort Information: www.sunvalley.com
Hailey, Idaho information: www.haileyid.areaguides.net/

Difficulty Ratings:
Easy: A typical beginner, fun, cruiser ride for most any ability.
Moderate: A bit harder than "easier" with most hills climbable, but not too technical.
Difficult: Fairly technical ride with tough climbs and descents. You will feel worked afterwards.
Abusive: The word speaks for itself, no matter the length of the ride. It is going to be hard, very technical, and you'll probably be in need of bandages.
Gonzo: In an effort to define a new category, this one is beyond abusive. This means bring gear for a bivy, extra food, matches, water and clothing.

Technical Ratings:
We rate our rides based on the technical aspect of it, as well. This rating is numbered from 1 to 5. 1 is the quite easy technically, while a ride rated with a 5 means it is very technical, so be mentally and physically prepared.

Ride Details:
Length: We would hope this is self-explanatory. However, all rides have cyclometer (mileage) readings. We also list as many features as possible so the people riding without a cyclometer won't get lost. In many cases, a GPS was also used to be sure ride stats are very accurate.
The Ride: Defines the ride as an out & back, loop or one-way.
Surface: Explains the riding surface.
Season: Tells you what time of year the ride is in it's best shape.
Fun Factor: Key words to describe the highlights of the ride.
Summary: Brief description of the ride to get you psyched up!

Tools/Clothing/Etc:

Hopefully, most of you are past getting dressed by your mothers each morning. Here is a small list of what to take just in case of some "interesting" weather.

Clothing: Rain or wind jacket, tights, gloves, cap, helmet, durable foot wear, and an extra fleece layer. Remember you are in the mountains here.

Tools: Extra tubes, pump, patches, chain tool, tire levers, allen wrenches, spoke wrench, screw driver (both kinds) and a small crescent wrench.

Misc. Items: More food and water than you think you need, first aid kit, emergency blanket and a camera (don't forget the film).

HELMET: ALWAYS, ALWAYS, ALWAYS!!!!!!!!!!!!!!!

Camping

Camping in the Sun Valley and Stanley area is relatively easy. There are pay campgrounds and there are "primitive" non-pay campgrounds. Most dirt roads off Highway 75 lead to some sort of primitive camping, while all of the pay campgrounds are labeled with official USFS signs. Most fees range anywhere from $7-$10 per day. All campgrounds limit your stay, so plan on leaving...eventually. If you're looking for a primitve campsite, take any dirt road north of Ketchum and you should be fine unless signs indicate otherwise. Please respect others and all private property.

Showers/Food/Hot Springs

So you stink and are hungry? No worries, we've got the places for you to chill out. Food, of course, is readily available in all the surrounding towns, as are motels, phones, etc. This is only as primitive as a place as you want it to be. Showers are available at a small cost in a couple areas: Redfish Lake, Easley Hot Springs, Sun Valley Athletic Club ($15...ouch!). Hot springs are dotted along the Salmon River north, west and east of Stanley, as well as up Warm Springs Road west of Ketchum. A special note on the hot springs: don't pee, poo, litter or detour the flow of or in any of the hot springs. Mother Nature put them here for us to enjoy, so please don't spoil it for the rest of the world.

Bugs & Animals

All of the rides in this guidebook are in the mountains where mosquitos, bees and other flying (stinging) insects live. Most repellents work great at knocking them off their wings. Be careful in the later part of summer for hornets and bees who tend to migrate toward open carbonated sugar drinks and beer. We also have a large population of big game animals. The elk, moose, deer, bear, wolf, fox, coyotes and all the other furry little creatures were here first. Remember that we are the ones playing in their homes and space. Please respect them and their privacy. Anyone caught harassing the animals will be stripped, tarred and feathered and paraded up and down main street in Ketchum on the hood of Johnny Law's car.

Idaho History & Wilderness

This part of central Idaho has a very rich history in mining. Around the lower part of the Wood River valley (Ketchum, Hailey, Bellevue), you can see mining scars, tailings and trails on the sides of some incredibly steep terrain. This is our mining past. Several rides in this guidebook lead to mining ghost towns such as Sawtooth City, Vienna, Custer, etc. In fact, back in the 1800's some of the populations of these mining communities were bigger than Ketchum is today.

In the Stanley area, prospectors and hermits were a big part of the scene. They made their living by trying to strike it rich with their mining claims or just living in the wilderness year-round on the Middle Fork of the Salmon River. These hearty people led a rugged lifestyle, usually seeing other humans only once or twice a year.

"The Wilderness State," is what Idaho is known as. We have somewhere around 12 to 13 million acres of wild lands around the state, ranging from National Forest to BLM to Wilderness areas to simple roadless areas. Idaho actually has more wild land areas than any of the other lower 48 states, excluding Alaska.

The Sawtooth Mountains, in the heart of the Sawtooth National Wilderness Area, are a huge attraction in the summertime benefiting backpackers, rock and alpine climbers as well as casual day hikers. However, these beautiful spires are not just for summer pleasure. They also offer great backcountry skiing in the winter and early springtime. But do take note: no mountain bikes or motorized vehicles are allowed in the Sawtooth Wilderness Area. So please respect the boundary signs and laws or Ranger Rick will be happy to do it for you. For more information on our local/state history, visit one of the bookstores in town. They all have a great selection.

Weather and Lightning

The mountains in the springtime can offer some of the most incredibly gorgeous scenery with wildflowers blooming and mountain streams flowing at full force. But don't be fooled by Mother Nature. June, July and August in central Idaho have a history of afternoon thunder storms that gather rapidly on the western horizon. Those small dark clouds in the distance can be upon you in no time, dumping rain, hail and even snow. So be prepared for anything. Always bring a rain jacket, extra food and water.

Another springtime worry in the mountains is lightning. "Oh, what are the chances," you ask? Actually, the chance of getting struck by lightning is very remote, but possible. Take all the necessary precautions when you begin to hear thunder and see lightning. Lightning is usually at the leading edge of a storm where it is most violent. If you are not sure that electricity is in the air, check some obvious signs.

Take your helmet off and if your hair is standing on end, then yes, there is electricity in the area. You can also check the hair on your arms and smell ozone in the air. Obvious question here, what does ozone smell like? Much different than the clear mountain air you've been breathing, almost like a wet dog (we're not kidding). If you get caught in an electric storm, do the following: make yourself small to minimize contact points with the ground (squat), get off any ridges, get away from lone trees, lake shores, and rock outcroppings. If someone is struck by lightning, (hopefully you know first aid) rush to get help. Due to the fact that we could get sued for telling you how to treat an injury, we can't say anything here.

Remember: DON'T GO OUT UNPREPARED FOR ANY EMERGENCY. You may be close to a town, but you are still miles away in a wild area and help can be just that much further away... "Be smart," as my dad would say.

Mountain Biking Ethics

The Authors Version: Do unto others as you would want them to do unto you and your bike. In other words, don't be a jerk on the trails. Yield to everyone, uphill traffic, horses, hikers and other cyclists. Treat our trails the way you eat in your mothers living room. Help out others in need of tools, water, etc. This isn't the World Cup or Olympics, this is a peaceful place, so chill out, put your adrenaline aside and relax.

The IMBA Version: Ride on open trails only. Leave no trace. Control your bicycle. Always yield the trail. Never spook Animals. Plan ahead.

DO NOT SKID, this deteriorates and erodes the trails making them use less. Push up or lower your bike down instead. Skidding around switchbacks is not the proper technique. Push your limits and when you reach the high end, push your bike.

DESCEND UNDER CONTROL to avoid skidding, trail erosion, hitting an other trail user and an expensive trip to the emergency room (remember 911).

STAY OFF WET TRAILS. This does not pertain to just "closed" trails in early season, since riding after a rain storm or snow melt can completely ruin a trail.

YIELD TO EVERYONE. Like it states above, this is a peaceful place we live in, so please be courteous to everyone or thing you encounter on the trails. Horses have very poor eyesight and are easily spooked. We have very poor eyesight and are easily spooked. Please be careful.

Other Activities

Welcome to resort town life where there are always activites happening to keep you busy when you're off the saddle or when it rains. There are four movie theatres between Ketchum and Hailey, bars everywhere, plenty of restaurants, horseback riding, world famous whitewater kayaking, paragliding, rafting and trails that offer great hiking to high alpine lakes. Don't forget your fishing gear. Fly-fishing is one of this areas main attractions. How about a round of golf on one of our world class golf courses? Remember this is a destination resort designed to keep you and your money happy.

More Websites of Interest

Idaho Website: www.visitidaho.org/
Idaho BLM: www.id.blm.gov/
Idaho State Parks: www.idahoparks.org/
Idaho High Desert: www.cihd.org/
Idaho Conservation League: www.wildidaho.org/
Idaho Sierra Club: www.sierraclub.org/id/
Trails Around the US: www.trails.com
International Mtn Biking Assoc: www.imba.com
DirtWorld: www.dirtworld.com/trails/
Pocatello Mtn Biking: www.isu.edu/outdoor/mtbike.htm
Tour de France: www.letour.fr

Iron Bog Lake in the Pioneer Mountains - McBob Collection

"Open your mind, open your life."

Please Sign In At The Trailheads

Please, please, please sign-in at ALL trailheads throughout the Wood River, Sawtooth and Copper Basin Valley's. The US Forest Service can close ANY trail to mountain biking if they feel it is not being used for that sport very much. Therefore, we need you to help make mountain bikers 'historical users' on all of these trails. The more the USFS sees mountain bikes being used, the less likely they are to close a trail. Please tell every mountain biker you see on the trails to sign in at the trailhead. Together, we can make a difference. That sounds familiar, must have heard it somewhere, sometime.

Want To Help With Our Trails?

Have you ever wanted to contribute either physically or financially to our extensive trail systems throughout the Wood River and Sawtooth Valley's? Well, now is your chance.

Good Dirt sponsors trail building and trail clean-up weekends and evenings throughout the summertime. If you would like to contribute your time or money, feel free to email us at: gmcbob@yahoo.com. We'll put you on a list of people to be called. If you can make it, great. If not, no worries, just send the pizza's and beer!

"Man Smart, (Woman Smarter)"
-Grateful Dead
(Read *"Stupid White Men"* if you need an explanation)

Riding in the South Valley Area

The first single-track in the entire area opens up in the South Valley area first. That usually means late March on a typical year, but mostly open by middle of April. Your best bet for early season riding is the south facing rides and dirt roads. As the season gets warmer, the riding gets a bit more dusty down there and can get increasingly hot as the days move on. Prepare for warmth and weather.

There are more and more trails being created in this area each season, so if you encounter a trail not mentioned on the ride list or overview map, chances are that it's a new one. Turn onto it and give it a roll, you never know where you'll end up, but chances are that you'll have an incredible time. In the more southern part of the valley are loads of jeep roads, especially out in the desert. These are phenomenal early season rides for getting the blood pumping back into your burned-out ski legs. Be careful out there by June, as the rattlers like to bask in and around the lava rocks!

Looking north on Hailey Main Street, circa 1920
Courtesy of Wood River Journal

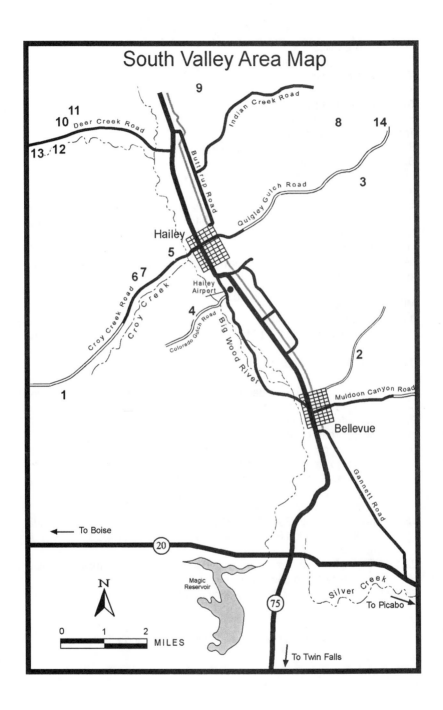

South Valley Area Map

1. Hatty Gulch

Length: 26.2 miles
Difficulty Rating: Moderate
Technical Rating: 2
The Ride: Loop
Starting Elevation: 5300'
High Point Elevation: 6000'
Total Elevation Gain: 1110'
Surface: Dirt jeep road, pavement, single track
Season: Late April - late November
Fun Factor: The serene sagebrush desert setting with cow pies, snakes and water.
Summary: This is the standard locals early season ride to get their legs and butt into shape. It's a fast cruise with a bit of climbing, mostly on jeep road.
Getting There: From Hailey Main Street, turn left (west) onto Bullion St at the street light and go 1.5 blocks to Hop Porter Park. This is where the ride begins. A shorter ride option is to drive to the junction with Rock Creek Road and begin the ride there.

Miles The Ride:

0.0 Begin by riding out Croy Creek on the pavement, passing through housing areas and the BMX track. Watch for Rotorun Ski Area on the right.

3.7 The pavement ends and the dirt road begins. Stay straight on this road.

4.1 Pass by Rock Creek Road on the left. Stay straight, this is where you complete the loop.

9.1 Just before starting to climb up Richardson Summit, turn left and follow this road down, passing by a "danger, open mines" sign.

9.3 Turn right on the switchback and follow the road down into the main gulch following the stream bed. You will follow this main Hatty Gulch all the way to the junction with Rock Creek Road. There may be new fencing, bad ruts and cows in your way, but stick to the road which follows the stream flow and you'll be fine.

18.5 The junction with Rock Creek Road. Turn left and begin some gradual climbing up toward Rocky Butte. Stay on this main road all the way up and over.

22.1 The junction with Croy Creek Road and your loop is complete. Follow Croy Creek Road back to Hailey.

26.2 Back at Hop Porter Park in Hailey and a job well done.

"Everything abides by the laws of cause and effect"

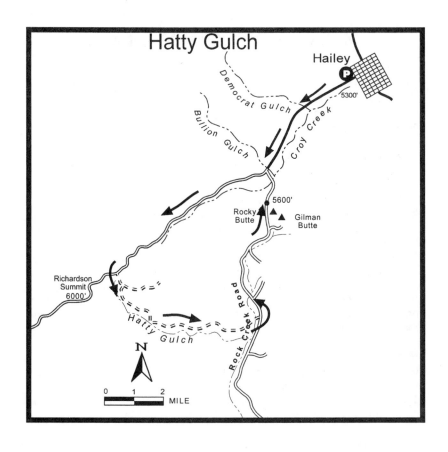

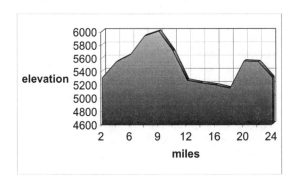

2. Slaughterhouse Creek

Length: 13 miles
Difficulty Rating: Easy
Technical Rating: 2 (creeks)
The Ride: Out & back
Starting Elevation: 5230'
High Point Elevation: 6200'
Total Elevation Gain: 970'
Surface: Dirt jeep road
Season: April - November
Fun Factor: Beautiful canyon with alpine meadows.
Summary: This is a casual ride through a southern canyon with alpine meadows, groves of aspens and five quick stream crossings (just to add a bit of excitement).
Getting There: From Hailey, drive south on Hwy 75 to Bellevue and turn east on Cedar Street, which is the street next to the old white building with a steeple that looks like an old church but is really the old Bellevue City Hall. Stay straight on this road, crossing the bike path and the elementary school on the left. Drive to the top of the hill and park anywhere out of the way of the road and driveways. The ride begins here.

Miles The Ride:

0.0 Begin by riding up the north side of the canyon.
0.2 Spur road on the right, stay straight.
1.4 Steep spur road takes off on the left which eventually hooks up with the spur road that takes off on the left at mile 1.5. Stay on the main road here.
2.7 A few springs muddy up the road a bit here (not bad). After some big shade trees, motor up a steep climb. From here the road crosses the creek five times over the next 2 miles.
4.8 You're at the last of the stream crossings.
5.0 Spur road up the canyon on the right, stay on the main road.
5.7 After the canyon narrows, it opens again fairly soon.
6.5 Fork in the road and the top of the ride for those of you joining us for the Out & Back portion of the movie. Those of you who want to call it good, turn around and ride the 6.5 miles back to the trailhead . . . thanks for playing. The left fork continues up the drainage (very rutted) to the saddle with Quigley Creek and down into Hailey. The right fork mean ders up to where it is too steep to ride. The ugly trail quickly turns to loose rocks and scree and ends at a small saddle with questionable views as to whether or not it's worth it. See the ride Quigley Creek to Slaughterhouse Creek for more information.
13.0 Back at your car in Bellevue.

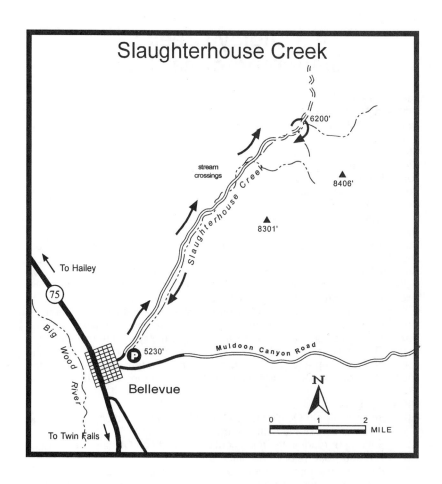

Slaughterhouse Creek

stream
crossings

Slaughterhouse Creek

6200'

▲
8406'

▲
8301'

To Hailey

75

Big Wood River

P 5230'

Muldoon Canyon Road

Bellevue

N

To Twin Falls

0   1   2
MILE

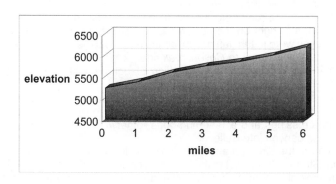

3. Quigley Creek to Slaughterhouse Creek

Length: 19.2 miles
Difficulty Rating: Moderate/Difficult
Technical Rating: 2+ (rutted downhill)
The Ride: Loop
Starting Elevation: 5350'
High Point Elevation: 6950'
Total Elevation Gain: 1600'
Surface: Dirt jeep road
Season: April - November
Fun Factor: Easy rolling ride through a southern canyon setting with good climbing.
Summary: This is a great non-technical ride with moderate elevation gain near the top end. If this were aerobics, it would be classified as "low impact."
Getting There: From the stop light at Bullion St and Hwy 75 in downtown Hailey, drive 1 block South to Croy Street and turn left here. After half a mile, follow the road around a natural right turn and take an immediate left onto Quigley Road, which is directly in front of the "Deerfield" sign. Continue forward to where the pavement turns to dirt and park here. **Please note that you can ride on single-track for quite a ways up Quigley right from the parking area. The single-track parallels the road to start and ends just before the pond, then starts up again to the right, just after the fence by the pond and goes to the corrals. Don't miss out on this fun part of the canyon!

Miles **The Ride:**

0.0 Begin riding up Quigley Creek Road heading east along side a large field and across the cattle guard.

2.2 Small spur road on the right, continue straight on Quigley Creek Road.

2.5 The spur road rejoins the main road.

4.2 Pass a corral then a spur road just a bit further on the left side.

5.8 Spur road on the left leads to/from Indian Creek. Continue up the main road curving to the south up and through some clear cuts. Always stay on the main road through this area.

7.8 At the fork in the road before a small creek (possibly dry in mid to late summer), turn right on the spur road, traversing back across the hill side. If you were to turn left or stay on the main road here, you would be on the *Quigley Creek to Cove Creek* ride.

8.3 You've reached the saddle overlooking Slaughterhouse Creek. Continue.

9.5 After crossing the small creek, stay to the right heading down the canyon toward Bellevue. For the next 6.5 miles you'll have many stream crossings and a few mud-bogs, otherwise it's a straight shot down the canyon into Bellevue.

16.0 The end of the dirt road and the town of Bellevue. Continue down Cedar Street until you get to the Wood River Bike Trail. Turn right. Ride approximately 3.2 miles into Hailey and turn right on Croy Street and retrace your steps to your car at the mouth of Quigley Creek.

19.2 End of the loop, and back at your car.

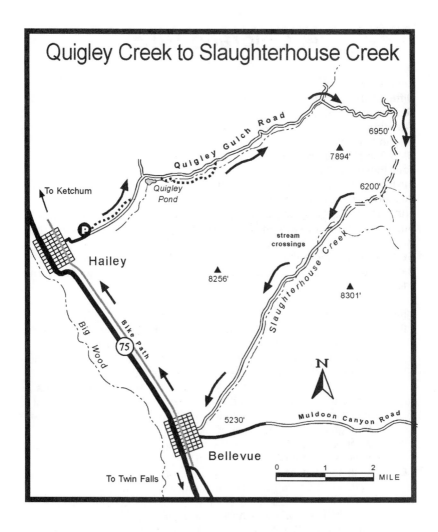

Quigley Creek to Slaughterhouse Creek

To Ketchum

Quigley Gulch Road

Quigley Pond

7894'

6950'

6200'

Hailey

stream crossings

Slaughterhouse Creek

8256'

8301'

Big Wood

Bike Path

75

N

Muldoon Canyon Road

5230'

Bellevue

To Twin Falls

0   1   2   MILE

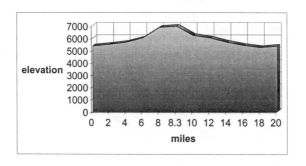

elevation

miles

4. Colorado Gulch

Length: 8.2 miles
Difficulty Rating: Moderate/Difficult
Technical Rating: 2+ (lungs)
The Ride: Loop
Starting Elevation: 5300'
High Point Elevation: 6250'
Total Elevation Gain: 950'
Surface: Dirt jeep road and pavement
Season: Mid-April - November
Fun Factor: A quick pump, a quick downhill and you're back on the couch.
Summary: If you have a need for a very quick workout to kill some of that daily stress, jump on this ride and pump 'til you puke!
Getting There: From the stop light at Bullion St and Hwy 75 in downtown Hailey, drive one block west (behind Pauls Grocery) to Hop Porter Park. The ride begins here.

Miles	The Ride:
0.0	Begin by riding back up to Main Street in Hailey (Hwy 75) and head south toward the airport. Turn right on Cedar St, just before the Post Office, then a quick left onto Broadford Rd. Go 0.8 miles and turn right on a dirt road (don't take the right just before the old abandoned wood house. Instead take the second, more beaten dirt road after the old wood house). Go down the road veering left and crossing the bridge over the Big Wood River and begin climbing through aspens next to the creek.
2.8	After passing several spur roads on either side of the road, pass a mine and old buildings on the left.
3.8	With some steady climbs behind you, the trail levels out for a spell before climbing again, and oh, baby does it climb!
4.1	Top of the ride. Congrats, catch your breath and get ready for a speedy ride downhill. Check your brakes first.
5.5	Junction with Croy Creek Road. Turn right (east) back toward Hailey, staying on Croy Creek Road.
8.2	Just after crossing the Big Wood River, you'll see Hop Porter Park on the left and your car. This is the end of the ride.

"Let go of whatever holds you back."

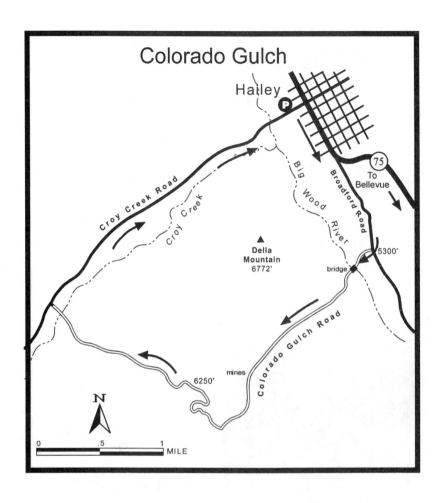

Colorado Gulch

Hailey

75
To
Bellevue

Croy Creek Road

Croy Creek

Big Wood River

Broadford Road

▲
Della
Mountain
6772'

5300'
bridge

Colorado Gulch Road

mines

6250'

N

0   .5   1
MILE

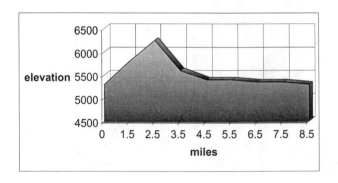

elevation

6500
6000
5500
5000
4500

0   1.5   2.5   3.5   4.5   5.5   6.5   7.5   8.5

miles

**DON'T FORGET TO EAT YOUR PASTA AT DAVINCI'S
THE NIGHT BEFORE THAT BIG RIDE**

Featuring New York Style
Italian Dinners
priced from $8.95 - $16.95

Open for Dinner
Wednesday - Sunday at 5pm
closed Monday and Tuesday

208-788-7699

**Located at 17 West Bullion St
1/2 block west of the Hailey stop light**

**Visit our Boise location - 190 E. State St - Downtown Eagle
208-939-2500**

5. Carbonate Mountain Trail

Length: 6.2 miles
Difficulty Rating: Moderate/Difficult
Technical Rating: 2+ (skinny trail and lungs)
The Ride: Out and back or loop option
Starting Elevation: 5300'
High Point Elevation: 6720'
Total Elevation Gain: 1420'
Surface: Single-track, dirt jeep road and pavement
Season: Late April - Early November
Fun Factor: Blow your lungs and legs out on a local 'test' piece with killer view.s
Summary: A fairly new trail in Hailey gets action early in the season, during lunch hours and post work for those dying to get a quick workout in legs and lungs!
Getting There: From the stop light at Bullion St and Hwy 75 in downtown Hailey, park 1 block behind Pauls Grocery Store at Hop Porter Park. The ride begins here.

Miles **The Ride:**

0.0 From the stop light in Hailey, head west on Bullion Street, quickly crossing over the Big Wood River.

0.1 You'll most likely see cars parked on the right side of the road next to the river and in front of a wooden fence. Lift your bike over the fence and start up the trail leading to the east and up.

0.2 Stay on the single-track which does NOT head straight up the ridge.

0.3 After a small climb, the trail now starts to switchback to the top.

2.1 The trail heads over the small saddle and crosses a jeep trail. Stay on the single-track as it switchbacks on the east side of the slope for a bit before heading back over to the south facing slopes.

2.8 The trail heads up the ridge, slightly steeper, but definitely doable.

3.1 The top of the ride and Carbonate Mountain. From here you can either turn around and go back down the way you came up. As another option, you could continue along the ridge trail heading north. Should you choose to go this way, go up at the powerlines and you just might find a little surprise of a single-track downhill at the end. Please be conscious of our bovine friends along the way.

6.2 Back down from Carbonate and back at your car, hopefully well-winded.

"Fall seven times, stand up eight"
-Japanese Proverb

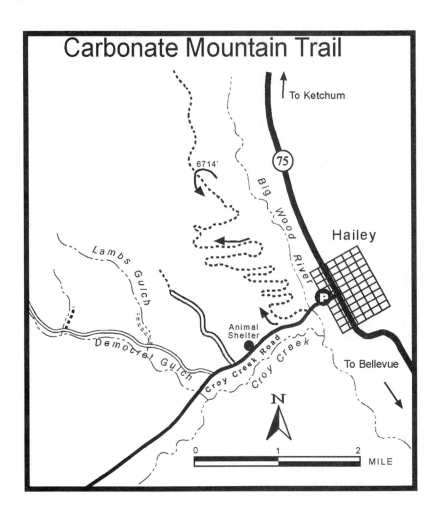

Carbonate Mountain Trail

To Ketchum

75

Big Wood River

6714'

Hailey

Lambs Gulch

Democrat Gulch

Animal Shelter

Croy Creek Road

Croy Creek

To Bellevue

N

0   1   2
MILE

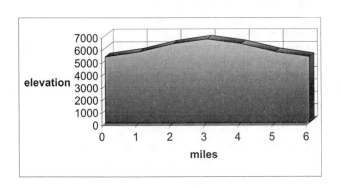

elevation

7000
6000
5000
4000
3000
2000
1000
0

0   1   2   3   4   5   6
miles

6. Democrat Gulch

Length: 12.4 miles
Difficulty Rating: Moderate/Difficult to top, or 'Easy' to first turn around.
Technical Rating: 2+ (rocks and lungs)
The Ride: Out and back
Starting Elevation: 5300'
High Point Elevation: 6750'
Total Elevation Gain: 750' or 1450' (750' to the first turn around)
Surface: Pavement to dirt jeep road
Season: Early April - late October
Fun Factor: Small but beautiful creek, Pioneer Mountain views, wildflowers.
Summary: So, you need a change of pace from that boring single-track riding? This is it. Casual or difficult, you make the choice, and either one is well worth it.
Getting There: From the stop light at Bullion St and Hwy 75 in downtown Hailey, park 1 block behind Pauls Grocery Store at Hop Porter Park. The ride begins here.

Miles **The Ride:**

0.0 From the stop light in Hailey, head west on Bullion Street, quickly crossing over the Big Wood River.

1.2 You are now in Croy Creek Canyon passing by the Wood River Animal Shelter.

1.7 Turn right onto Democrat Gulch road and wind up the side of a small hill. There may or may not be other cars parked at this make-shift trailhead.

2.0 A gravel road enters in from the left. Stay on main road heading north.

2.9 Spur road on the right goes up Lamb's Gulch. Notice a small pond on the left. Remember, stay on the main road.

3.9 Spur road on the right, don't take it.

4.1 Beaver ponds on the left.

4.7 Enter into the rocky corridor, you'll know what we mean.

5.0 Cross over the creek on an exposed pipe.

5.2 Fork in the road after crossing over the creek. The left road goes no where. Take the right fork and begin a gradual climb to the top. This can also be a turn-around point for the more casual version of this ride, otherwise continue on up. (6050')

6.2 This is the top of the ride. You can check out the Pioneer Mountains to the East, or explore the other trails up here. Be careful descending back down the gulch and into Hailey. **The trail heading down the north-side of this saddle leads to private property in Deer Creek. Please do not go down.

12.4 Back in Hailey and the end of the ride.

"When the cyclist is ready, the trail will appear"
-Modified Buddhist Proberb

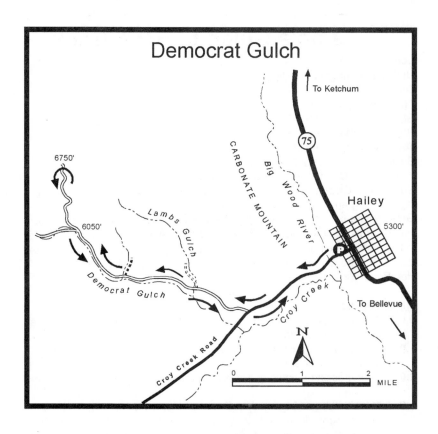

Democrat Gulch

To Ketchum

75

6750'

CARBONATE MOUNTAIN

Big Wood River

Lambs Gulch

6050'

Hailey

5300'

P

Democrat Gulch

Croy Creek

To Bellevue

N

Croy Creek Road

0   1   2
MILE

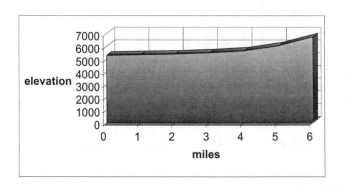

7. Lamb's Gulch to BMX Track

Length: 8.4 miles
Difficulty Rating: Moderate
Technical Rating: 2+
The Ride: Loop
Starting Elevation: 5300'
High Point Elevation: 6220'
Total Elevation Gain: 1050'
Surface: Dirt jeep road, single-track, pavement
Fun Factor: Good for early season and late fall in a peaceful setting.
Summary: Close to Hailey single-track that'll get your heart pounding, your legs burning and a smile on your face.
Getting There: From the stop light at Bullion St and Hwy 75 in downtown Hailey, drive west into the large canyon aptly named Croy Canyon. At 1.7 miles, park on the right side of the road next to the dirt road and fence. Please don't block the road. The ride begins here. **You could also start this ride at Hop Porter Park in Hailey by the river.

Miles The Ride:

0.0 Begin by riding up the dirt road (quick hill) that you parked next to. Stay on this road for the next 1 mile.

1.0 Turn right just past the trees onto a jeep road which crosses the stream soon thereafter.

2.0 After crossing a cattle guard then another stream, stay left at the next junction.

2.5 In the small clearing a jeep road goes up and left and a jeep road goes up and right. Instead, take the single-track which follows along the right side of the creekbed. After roughly 0.2 miles, take a sharp left turn in the aspens and begin a meandering climb up to the top.

2.9 At the saddle where the trails all join up, turn right (west) and head down on a faint jeep trail which turns to single-track shortly. On the grassy hill, make your way down the semi-non-existent trail to the grove of trees. There, you will find a better single-track trail leading left into the trees and down the canyon on the _east_ side of the creek.

3.8 Junction with Democrat Gulch Road. Turn right here.

3.9 Whoa! Look for the single-track dropping down to the left and crossing the creek, which is located where the willows are closest to the road.

4.3 The top of the first saddle. The trail forks shortly afterwards. Both trails lead to the same place a hundred yards later, but be careful of loose rocks.

4.9 Cross over the dry stream bed and follow the faint trail leading left and up.

5.1 Top of the second saddle. Careful for the sharp turn on the descent.

5.6 In the clearing with houses down to the left, stay straight and continue traversing up on the double track jeep road.

5.8 Top of the last saddle overlooking the BMX track area. There are many trails all over the place as you descend. Stay on the most popular path, which veers left and east across the back of the BMX track.

6.5 Junction with Croy Creek Road. Turn left and follow this road back to your car at the start of Democrat Gulch.

8.4 Yep, you're here, the end of the ride. Nice job!

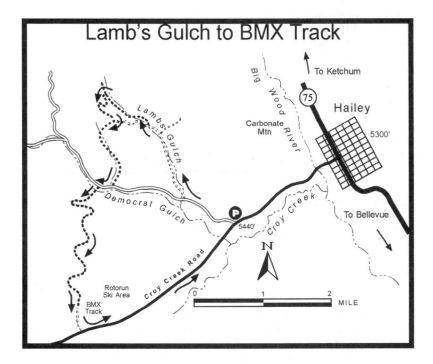

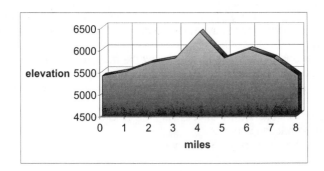

8. Quigley Creek to Indian Creek

Length: 19.2 miles
Difficulty Rating: Moderate/Difficult
Technical Rating: 2+ (loose scree coming down Indian Crk)
The Ride: Loop
Starting Elevation: 5397'
High Point Elevation: 7310'
Total Elevation Gain: 1913'
Surface: Pavement and dirt jeep road
Season: Late April - October
Fun Factor: Fun hill-climbs, killer views and an awesome descent!
Summary: This can be as intense as you make it. Stop often on the climb and enjoy yourself, or abuse yourself and do it non-stop. Once the climb is over, this is an amazing downhill all the way back to Hailey.
Getting There: From the stop light in downtown Hailey, drive south one block and turn left (east) on Croy St. Follow all the way as it bends to the right, then take a quick left onto Quigley Road. Follow Quigley Road until it turns to dirt. Park on the left. **Please note that you can ride on single-track for quite a ways up Quigley right from the parking area. The single-track parallels the road to start and ends just before the pond, then starts up again to the right, just after the fence by the pond and goes to the corrals. Don't miss out on this fun part of the canyon!

Miles The Ride:

0.0   Begin riding up Quigley Creek Road heading east along side a large field and across the cattle guard.
1.75 Pass the Quigley Pond on the right side of the road.
2.2   Small spur road on the right, continue straight on Quigley Creek Road.
2.5   The spur road rejoins the main road.
4.2   Pass a corral then a spur road just a bit further on the left side.
5.8   Turn left at the fork which leads to Indian Creek.
6.0   Begin slowly climbing up the canyon. Pace yourself!
8.5   Spur road to the left. Don't take it, it leads to private property.
8.8   The top of the climbing. Take in the views and breathe. Descend the main road all the way to pavement. Take note, there are side roads on the way.
13.0 Dirt ends and pavement begins. Follow the main road all the way down Indian Creek until the junction with Buttercup Road.
16.2 Buttercup Road. Cross over it and ride on the bike path heading south.
18.2 Bike path intersects Croy Street. Turn left on Croy Street and retrace your steps back to your car.
19.2 Your car. You're worked. You're happy?!

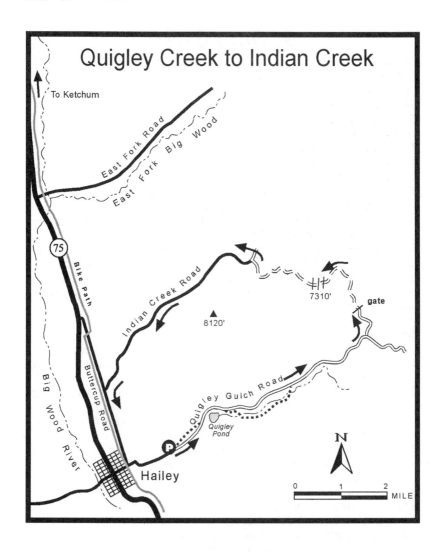

Quigley Creek to Indian Creek

To Ketchum

East Fork Road

East Fork Big Wood

75

Bike Path

Indian Creek Road

8120'

7310'

gate

Big Wood River

Buttercup Road

Quigley Gulch Road

Quigley Pond

P

Hailey

N

0   1   2
MILE

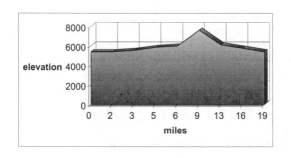

9. Ohio Gulch

Length: 14.6 miles
Difficulty Rating: Moderate/Difficult
Technical Rating: 1
The Ride: Out and back
Starting Elevation: 5620'
High Point Elevation: 7870'
Total Elevation Gain: 2250'
Surface: Dirt jeep road
Season: Late April - October
Fun Factor: Great views, beautiful canyon setting and a killer pump!
Summary: If you're in the mood for a nice evening or morning pump, this is the ride for you. Beautiful views of the Ohio Gulch Transfer Station (county dump), and the Pioneer and Smoky Mountains.
Getting There: From Ketchum, drive South on Hwy 75 for 6.8 miles and turn left on Ohio Gulch Rd. Immediately park on the right side of the road in the gravel next to the bike path. This is where the ride begins. (*You can also drive up Ohio Gulch Road the 1.8 miles to where the gravel road begins and skip the pavement portion of the ride.)

Miles The Ride:

0.0 Ride up the paved Ohio Gulch Rd heading toward the foothills.
1.0 The Gun Club appears on the left. Stay on the road toward the transfer station.
1.8 The Transfer station turn off is on the left. Keep straight and continue onto the gravel road which begins weaving around and behind the transfer station. The right fork leads overland to Indian Creek subdivision.
2.9 View point of the upper transfer station and beginning of a quick rocky downhill. At the bottom of the downhill, continue on the main jeep road to the right.
3.2 Gain a small saddle and prepare for some climbing ahead.
3.8 Encounter a small steep hill which is a tough climb.
4.1 Begin a scree-slope hill climb, one of a series to come.
4.3 Gain another small saddle and get ready to climb again.
5.0 The first of a few switchbacks starts here with moderate to easy climbing between them.
5.9 Come into a clearing with awesome views of the Smokey Mountains to the West. Continue up a series of switchbacks and moderate climbing with a steep hill climb to gain the summit saddle.
7.3 The top! Incredible views of the Pioneer Mountains and the canyons of Indian and Quigley creeks. Take some pictures, suck in some air, enjoy the views and get ready for a fast downhill! There is a small single-track leading off to the east which goes around the small knob. It eventually leads down into Indian Creek area and/or Cove Creek drainage.
14.6 End of the ride and (hopefully) back to your car.

Ohio Gulch

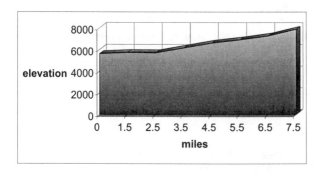

10. North Fork of Deer Creek

Length: 11.3 miles
Difficulty Rating: Difficult
Technical Rating: 4 (all on the descent)
The Ride: Loop
Starting Elevation: 5970'
High Point Elevation: 7440'
Total Elevation Gain: 1470'
Surface: Dirt jeep road and single track trail
Season: Early June - late October
Fun Factor: Beautiful creeks, wildflowers, and high alpine meadows.
Summary: The best part of this ride is getting the climbing done first and having a killer downhill for over 6+ miles. Killer views and tons of wildlife!
Getting There: From Ketchum, drive south on Hwy 75 for 10.9 miles and turn right at the forest service sign for "Deer Creek Road." Follow this road for just over 10 miles to the junction with "North Fork of Deer Creek" and park on the left off the road at this junction. This is where the ride begins.

<u>Miles</u> <u>The Ride</u>:

0.0   Begin by riding up the N. Fork Deer Creek Road.

1.6   Take the left fork at the trailhead leading up a single track trail.

4.0   The top of the ride at the trail junction. Continue on down the other side toward Poison Flats. The right fork leads to Mars Ridge.

4.4   A small pond is located in the trees here. Not good swimming, but good wildlife viewing possibilities.

4.9   Trail junction. Take the left fork leading down the Deer Creek drainage. The right fork goes toward Poison Flats.

9.0   Pass by Curran Gulch trailhead on the right. Stay on the main trail down.

10.1   Primitive hunting campsite and the start of the jeep road and the end of the single track.

10.7   Pass by the Kinsey Creek trailhead on the right. Stay on the jeep road down.

11.3   You just rode past your car. Hey, hey, turn around, that was the end of the ride.

"Those who have not asked the question,
are not ready to accept the answer"

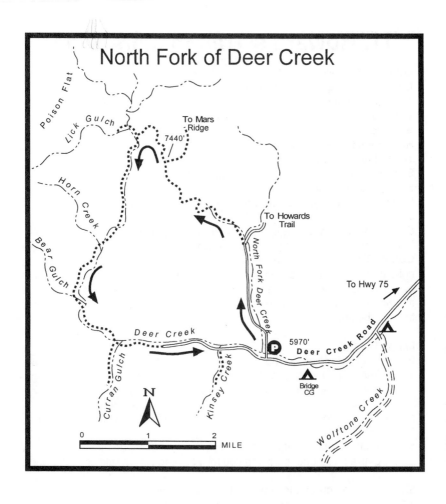

North Fork of Deer Creek

Poison Flat

Lick Gulch

To Mars Ridge

7440'

Horn Creek

To Howards Trail

Bear Gulch

North Fork Deer Creek

To Hwy 75

Deer Creek

5970'

Deer Creek Road

P

Curran Gulch

Kinsey Creek

Bridge CG

N

Wolftone Creek

0   1   2   MILE

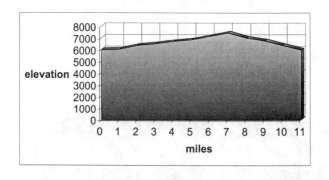

11. Howard's Trail to Mars Ridge

Length: 12.1 miles
Difficulty Rating: Difficult/Abusive
Technical Rating: 3+
The Ride: Loop
Starting Elevation: 6360'
High Point Elevation: 8525'
Total Elevation Gain: 2165'
Surface: Dirt jeep road and single track trail
Season: June - late October
Fun Factor: 360 degree views of the entire area, wildflowers and a moon-scape.
Summary: This is an aerobic ride with some grinding and killer downhills. Bring extra food, water, a jacket and a camera. You'll want and use them all!
Getting There: From Ketchum, drive south on Hwy 75 for 10.9 miles and turn right at the forest service sign for "Deer Creek Road." Follow this road for just over 10 miles to the junction with "North Fork of Deer Creek". Turn right for another 1.6 miles and park on the left near the trailhead sign. This is where the ride begins.

Miles The Ride:

0.0 Begin by riding up the jeep road following the sign to Howard's Trail.

1.3 The jeep road ends at a small creek crossing. From here it's all single track up the switchbacks to the next junction. All rideable, never too steep.

3.9 The junction with Greenhorn Gulch. Turn left and continue climbing up.

5.0 Another junction at a saddle. Turn left and continue more climbing. It gets a bit steeper here and you may have to walk a little bit. Well worth it!

5.7 You are now on the famous Mars Ridge, enjoy the scenery and ride on.

7.3 Now that you're done riding along the ridge, at the junction, turn left and start the descent into the North Fork of Deer Creek.

8.6 You now drop into the trees leaving the upper bowl and ridge behind.

9.8 Junction with North Fork of Deer Creek trail. Turn left (south) and begin an incredibly fun switchback descent (that is if you didn't think the past 2 miles have been a hoot!). **You could also turn right and complete the remainder of the North Fork of Deer Creek ride.

12.1 The single track has ended right at your car. Wow, that was awesome!

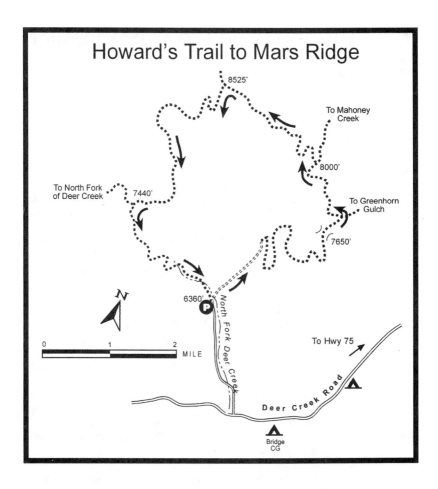

Howard's Trail to Mars Ridge

8525'

To Mahoney Creek

8000'

To North Fork of Deer Creek

7440'

To Greenhorn Gulch

7650'

6360'

North Fork Deer Creek

To Hwy 75

0   1   2   MILE

Deer Creek Road

Bridge CG

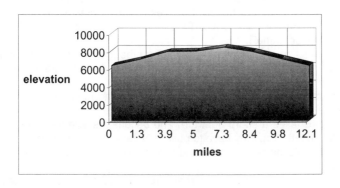

10000
8000
6000
elevation
4000
2000
0

0   1.3   3.9   5   7.3   8.4   9.8   12.1

miles

12. Wolftone Creek to Curran Gulch

Length: 18.4 miles
Difficulty Rating: Difficult
Technical Rating: 3+
The Ride: Loop
Starting Elevation: 5850'
High Point Elevation: 7800'
Total Elevation Gain: 1950'
Surface: Dirt jeep road and single track trail
Season: June - October
Fun Factor: Views, views and more views.
Summary: This ride rivals any in the area for fun, challenge and views. (*Another option for this ride is to ride to the saddle next to Kelly Mountain and down into Croy Creek. The turn off for that ride is at mile 5 listed below).
Getting There: From Ketchum, drive south on Hwy 75 for approximately 9 miles and turn right at the forest service sign for "Deer Creek Road." Follow this road for just over 8 miles and park on the left by the sign indicating Wolftone Creek.

Miles The Ride:

0.0   Begin the ride by heading up Wolftone Creek Road.

1.1   After gaining a small hill on mining tailings, follow the road as it turns west and heads up the canyon.

2.7   Spur road and a cabin on the right leads nowhere too exciting. Continue to ride forward.

3.9   End of the road and beginning of single track trail. Continue riding up the valley. DO NOT take the trail which crosses the creek and switches back to the left. Stay right and go straight up the drainage.

4.4   At the fork, stay right. From here the trail crosses the creek several times. Always stay on the main trail.

5.0   Just after a creek crossing you encounter a road going both left and right. Turn right here and begin a pleasant cruise up and through the trees. (*If going to Croy Creek from here, turn left to the Kelly Mountain saddle at the top. Use common sense in directions going down the other side. Its approximately 4.5 miles to Croy Creek Road and 16 miles into Hailey. Use USGS Topo map "Mahoney Butte" and "Richardson Butte").

5.4   After crossing a small creek, continue up the main road. Do not turn left on the faint single track. From here the road is a bit steep and loose.

6.3   The first of many saddles is reached. Follow the road down a bit before starting some serious climbing.

6.8   The road takes a sharp right turn and becomes single track climbing up to the left. You may have to push a bit here, but hang in there. It mellows in a bit before traversing over to the saddle above Kinsey Creek.

8.1   The saddle on top of Kinsey Creek. You can either drop into Kinsey Creek for a shorter loop, or continue on into Curran Gulch. The details of the rest of this ride are listed under the *Kinsey Creek to Curran Gulch*.

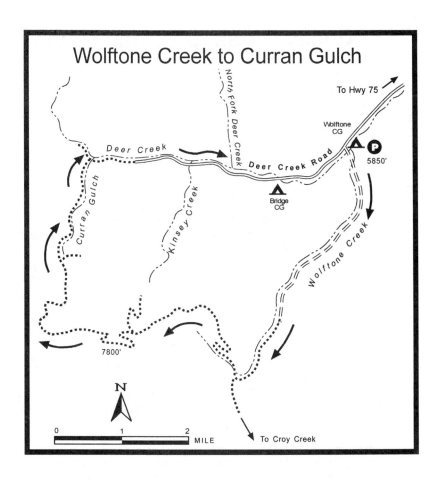

Wolftone Creek to Curran Gulch

To Hwy 75

North Fork Deer Creek

Wolftone CG

Deer Creek

Deer Creek Road

5850'

Curran Gulch

Kinsey Creek

Bridge CG

Wolftone Creek

7800'

N

0   1   2
MILE

To Croy Creek

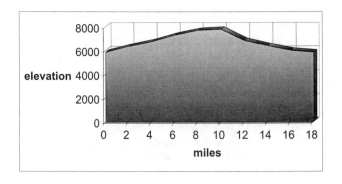

elevation

13. Kinsey Creek to Curran Gulch

Length: 10.4 miles
Difficulty Rating: Difficult
Technical Rating: 3+
The Ride: Loop
Starting Elevation: 6040'
High Point Elevation: 7800'
Total Elevation Gain: 1760'
Surface: Dirt jeep road and single track trail.
Season: Early June - October
Fun Factor: Adventure ride, views, route finding, views, route...
Summary: This isn't as bad as the elevation gain seems, but it is still a grinder. Once up, it's a great run down. Fairly sandy on the way up and technical on the way down.
Getting There: From Ketchum, drive south on Hwy 75 for approximately 9 miles and turn right at the forest service sign for "Deer Creek Road." Follow this road for 11.5 miles and park next to the unsigned Kinsey Creek coming into the canyon from the left. Park somewhere near by, but please don't block the road.

Miles The Ride:

0.0   Begin by riding through Deer Creek then up the trail into the Kinsey Creek drainage.

1.2   Pass by a trail leading off to the right which eventually leads into the Curran Gulch drainage. Stay on the main trail passing by a spur road on the left.

1.5   At the fork in the road, take the left and more heavily travelled road which crosses the creek. From here you begin a long climb.

3.5   The top of the saddle. From here the trail gets a bit more interesting. Straight ahead leads into Croy Creek and left leads to Wolftone Creek. Instead, turn right at the top of the saddle and ride for roughly 50+ feet on a primitive trail, before jumping off to the left on a trail which descends quickly to a road about 50 yards below. Yes, it is the trail if you go literally straight down the hill. Turn right onto the road and follow it for one mile, where it starts to switchback to the right and climb.

4.5   After rounding the switchback, continue for a couple hundred yards. Look to your left for a very easy trail to miss leading off to the left traversing the ridge. **DO NOT MISS THIS TURN.

5.5   After gaining the final ridge-top, the trail becomes a bit of a roller-coaster as it drops its way into Curran Gulch.

7.3   You'll come to a trail junction with a trail coming in from Kinsey Creek. Stay straight and continue down the drainage.

8.8   After crossing over Deer Creek, meet up with the Deer Creek Trail and turn right, heading down the drainage.

9.8   Ride past the official trailhead for the Deer Creek Trail and enter into a hunters camp and on to a dirt jeep road. Continue down the road.

10.4 The end of the ride and back at the Kinsey Creek trailhead.

Kinsey Creek to Curran Gulch

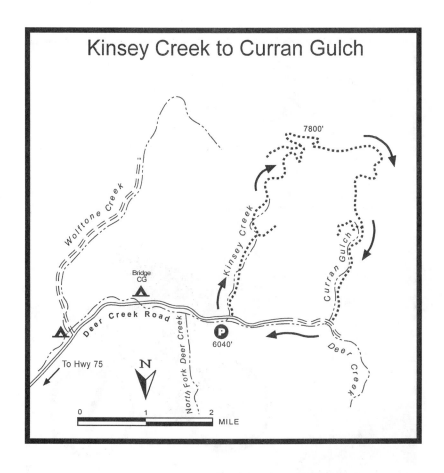

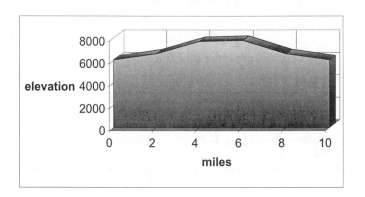

14. Quigley Creek to Cove Creek

Length: 31.1 miles
Difficulty Rating: Moderate/Difficult
Technical Rating: 2
The Ride: Loop
Starting Elevation: 5350'
High Point Elevation: 7250'
Total Elevation Gain: 1900'

Surface: Dirt road, single-track, pavement
Season: Late April - late October
Fun Factor: Pioneer mountain views, wildlife and solitude.
Summary: Whether you shuttle a car to Triumph or make a loop out of it, this is a wonderful ride for most anyone. Due to the length, it will leave you with a good thigh burn. High alpine meadows, aspens and the occasional elk or antelope just add to the experience.
Getting There: From Main Street in Hailey, turn east on Croy Street and follow the road as it takes a natural right turn. Turn left on Quigley Road at the "Deerfield" sign. Follow that street until it joins up with a dirt road heading up the canyon approximately one-half mile later. Park here. **Please note that you can ride on single-track for quite a ways up Quigley right from the parking area. The single-track parallels the road to start and ends just before the pond, then starts up again to the right, just after the fence by the pond and goes to the corrals. Don't miss out on this fun part of the canyon!

Miles The Ride:

0.0 Begin riding up Quigley Creek Road heading east along side a large field and across the cattle guard.

1.75 Pass the Quigley Pond on the right side of the road.

2.2 Small spur road on the right, continue straight on Quigley Creek Road.

2.5 The spur road rejoins the main road.

4.2 Pass a corral then a spur road just a bit further on the left side.

5.8 Spur road on the left leads to/from Indian Creek. Continue up the main road curving to the south up and through some clear cuts. Always stay on the main road through this area.

7.6 Small private cabin appears off to the right.

7.7 Spur road and switchback leads off to the right which heads over and down to Slaughterhouse Creek and into Bellevue. Instead stay on the main road crossing over a small creek bed (possibly dry in mid to late summer) and heading northeast.

8.6 Saddle in a mud bog area. Take the first left heading down the canyon to the northeast and left. Do not turn right, it leads nowhere.

9.1 After a bit of a rutted downhill, a road takes off to the left just before a muddy creek crossing. Stay on the main road through the muddy crossing.

9.4 Take a left on the grassy double-track . . . trust me.

10.1 Take another left and go down the hill.

10.4 Yes, go left again and begin the famous Narrows single-track trail.

11.7 The Narrows ends at the Cove Creek Road. Go right and toward the beaver ponds, heading north.

12.6 A fun descent leads to a junction with another main road. Go right here passing by the beaver ponds and a spur road on the right. Continue on down the main road.

13.7 Pass by Hook Draw on the right.

14.2 Small spur road on the left leads to nowhere.

16.2 Major junction here. This is East Fork Road. Turn left here.

17.2 Spur road off to the right leads to Hyndman Creek and the Pioneer Mountains main "peak" district.

18.5 Pavement and the town of Triumph. If you shuttled a car here, this is the end of your ride. If you're bumming there's no car here, continue down the paved East Fork Road.

24.4 Turn left before Hwy 75 and head south on the paved bike path.

30.6 As the bike path comes into Hailey, follow it to Croy Street and turn left here retracing your route back to your car.

31.1 Back at your car at Quigley Canyon and the end of the ride.

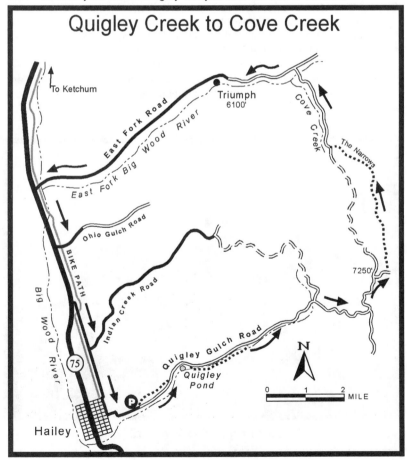

Quigley Creek to Cove Creek

Riding Around the Ketchum Area:

Mountain biking around Ketchum over the past 10 years has become a mecca for enthusiasts, coming from both far and wide. The area is not spoken about in terms of a Moab or Fruita, as most people who come to Ketchum don't like to tell others of their find. Once you've ridden around Ketchum, undoubtedly you'll be coming back for your pilgrimage to mecca year after year.

The trails here have been compared to a smooth brown carpet surrounded by pine trees. We even heard one visitor from out of state say, "I heard that everyone gets together in Ketchum and sweeps the trails." Yes, the trails are smooth and velvety, but not THAT smooth and velvety, so don't expect a miracle, but you will be impressed.

Most visitors to the area tend to congregate at the Adams Gulch Area, due to it's proximity to Ketchum, as do the lunchtime locals needing a quick aerobic fix. However, there are SO many other places to go play around the immediate area that are equally, if not better: Greenhorn Gulch Area, Deer Creek Area, Galena Lodge Area.

While riding around the Ketchum area, one place not to forget is the Bald Mountain Trails. You can either ride up the lift and just do a downhill, or ride up and down on the trails. Either way is a blast.

Regardless of where you ride around the area, you're sure to have a smile on your face at the end of the day. Don't be afraid to ask other riders questions or suggestions for other trails to ride, as most everyone is friendly and will offer great advice.

Ketchum, Idaho, circa 1910
courtesy of Wood River Journal

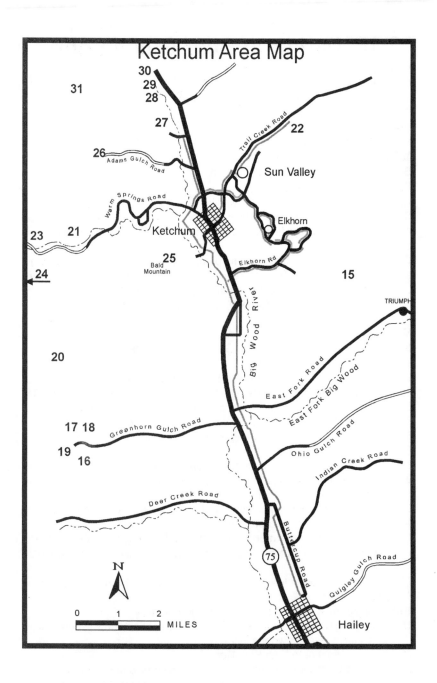

Ketchum Area Map

31

30
29
28

27

Trail Creek Road

22

26
Adams Gulch Road

Warm Springs Road

Sun Valley

○

Elkhorn
○

23   21

Ketchum

24 ←

25
Bald
Mountain

Elkhorn Rd

15

TRIUMPH

Big Wood River

20

East Fork Road

East Fork Big Wood

17 18
Greenhorn Gulch Road

19
16

Ohio Gulch Road

Indian Creek Road

Deer Creek Road

Buttercup Road

N

0   1   2
MILES

75

Quigley Gulch Road

Hailey

46

15. Parker to Bear Gulch Loop

Length: 20.8 miles
Difficulty Rating: Difficult
Technical Rating: 3 (mainly going up Parker)
The Ride: Loop
Starting Elevation: 6005"
High Point Elevation: 8610"
Total Elevation Gain: 2605'
Surface: Dirt jeep road and single track
Season: Late May - October
Fun Factor: Pioneer Mountain views like you've never seen before.
Summary: You'll burn your lungs and pound your legs, all for the most amazing views and wildlife everywhere! This is a must-do ride if ya think ya can handle it!
Getting There: From Ketchum, drive south on Hwy 75 to East Fork Road, approximately 5 miles. Turn left (east) here and drive approximately 5 miles and park on the left where a major dirt jeep road takes off. This is where the ride begins. If you went to Triumph, turn around 1 mile to the starting point.

Miles The Ride:

0.0	Begin by riding up Triumph Gulch on a fairly major jeep road.
1.5	At the fork, stay left here.
2.9	Round a saddle with views of Elkhorn and the valley below.
4.2	Go screaming by Independence Mine. DO NOT GO INTO ANY SHAFTS!
5.5	Jeep road ends at pavement above The Ranch at Elkhorn condos.
6.1	At the stop sign, go right.
6.7	Again, at the stop sign go right. This is the beginning of Parker Gulch Road.
8.5	The gravel road now becomes double track jeep road.
9.4	In the big grassy meadow, stay left and you'll find the trail again. It is single-track from here on up.
9.9	The switchbacks begin. Now is when you need those lungs and legs!
11.4	The first saddle, hold on, there's more...
12.0	The top of the ride at 8610', overlooking Uncle John's Gulch to the north and Bear Gulch to the south. To the east are the Pioneer Mountains.
12.5	A small saddle before really dropping into Bear Gulch. Stay left at the fork.
15.5	Single track ends at a double track jeep road.
15.7	Junction with Hydeman Creek Road, stay right and down. You'll follow this all the way down the valley.
18.6	Take a right onto East Fork Road.
19.8	The town of Triumph. Watch for kids and cruise through town.
20.8	Back at your car and the end of another awesome ride!

Parker-Bear Gulch Loop

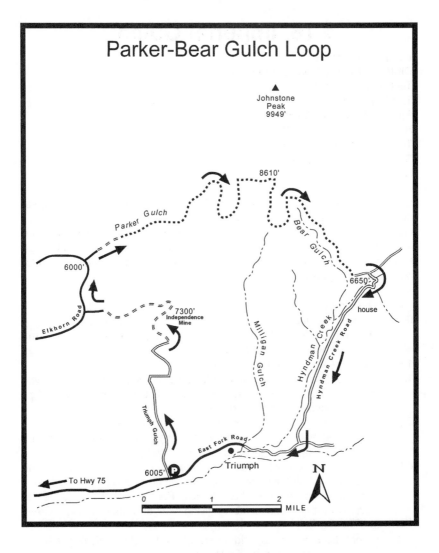

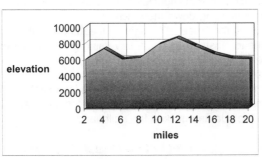

16. Imperial Gulch

Length: 10.5 miles
Difficulty Rating: Moderate/Difficult
Technical Rating: 2+
The Ride: Loop
Starting Elevation: 5900'
High Point Elevation: 7450'
Total Elevation Gain: 1550'
Surface: Single track trail
Season: May - October
Fun Factor: Scenic, fun loop and incredible downhill.
Summary: With a grind up Greenhorn Gulch, you are rewarded with a great descent into Imperial Gulch with views, flowers, wildlife and more views.
Getting There: From Ketchum, drive south on Hwy 75 for 6 miles and turn west (right) at the light onto Greenhorn Gulch Road. Follow the road through Golden Eagle Subdivision to the end of the road, and follow the dirt road for half mile to the parking lot. The ride begins here.

Miles The Ride:

0.0 Follow the trail exiting the parking lot area on the west side. The beginning of this trail is quite rocky and rough, but don't let this turn you off, it becomes great at the top.

1.0 Pass by Cow Creek Trail on the right.

1.4 Trail junction: Right trail leads to Mahoney Creek and Lodgepole Creek, but turn left and continue up toward Deer Creek, gradually climbing through pines next to the stream.

3.8 You see an unsigned trail on the right leads up Mahoney Creek, but continue straight on the main trail heading toward Deer Creek with casual climbing through beautiful pines alongside the creek.

4.9 You encounter a trail junction at the saddle. From here take a hard left, passing by a trail exiting off to the right and down into Deer Creek. This is the beginning of Imperial Gulch Trail. For the next 2.7 miles the trail traverses with minimal climbing giving wonderful views of Deer Creek and the Mahoney Creek drainages.

7.6 Whoa! Be sure and turn right here where the sign indicates "trail."

8.1 Faint trail leading off to the right leads into Deer Creek. Stay straight on the main trail heading down the gulch.

8.8 Trail junction at the fence. The right trail leads to another Imperial Gulch trailhead. Instead, turn left, traversing gradually up and to a saddle over looking Greenhorn Gulch.

9.3 The saddle. Continue on down the trail.

10.3 The bottom of the Imperial Gulch Trail at the intersection with Greenhorn Gulch. Turn right and continue back to the trailhead.

10.5 The end of the ride and back at the trailhead.

(This trail is sponsored by Base Mountain Properties)

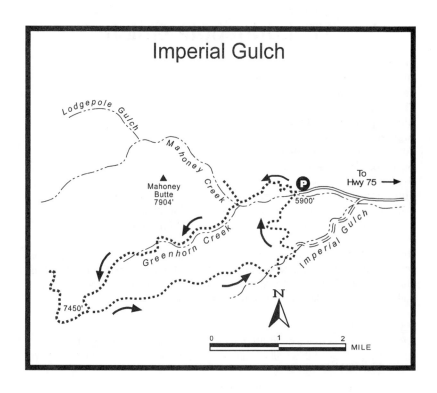

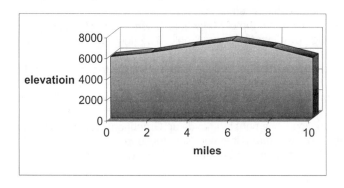

17. Lodgepole Gulch

Length: 11.9 miles
Difficulty Rating: Moderate/Difficult
Technical Rating: 2
The Ride: Loop
Starting Elevation: 5900'
High Point Elevation: 7850'
Total Elevation Gain: 1950'
Surface: Single track trail
Season: May - late October
Fun Factor: Wildflowers, climbing, great downhill, meadows.
Summary: This whole area is a great place for riding, no matter which loop you do. Lodgepole Gulch is known for its great downhills and moderate climbs.
Getting There: From Ketchum, drive south on Hwy 75 for 6 miles and turn west (right) at the light onto Greenhorn Gulch Road. Follow the road through Golden Eagle Subdivision to the end of the road, and follow the dirt road for half mile to the parking lot. The ride begins here.

Miles The Ride:

0.0 Follow the trail exiting the parking lot area on the west side. The beginning of this trail is quite rocky and rough, but don't let this turn you off.

1.0 Pass by Cow Creek Trail on the right.

1.4 Trail junction: Turn right toward Mahoney Creek Trail and Lodgepole Trail and begin a gradual ascent.

3.7 You reach a trail junction. Turn right and into Lodgepole Gulch. From here you climb about 1000' feet over the next 2.1 miles. It is never too hard, so take many deep breaths, endure the grind and relax and enjoy the beautiful scenes.

5.8 Trail junction at the top of Lodgepole Gulch. Turn left and begin descending down into Mahoney Creek. The right trail leads into Red Warrior Creek.

6.7 Trail junction: The right fork leads to the top of Mahoney Creek, instead, turn left and down the drainage.

8.4 Trail junction: The left fork leads back up into Lodgepole Gulch, instead, turn right and down heading back to the trailhead.

10.5 Trail junction: The right fork leads up Greenhorn Gulch and into Deer Creek. Instead, turn left to complete the loop.

11.9 The end of the ride and back at the trailhead.

"Looking for lasting happiness outside yourself is meaningless.
It is like expecting to become fit by watching other people exercise."

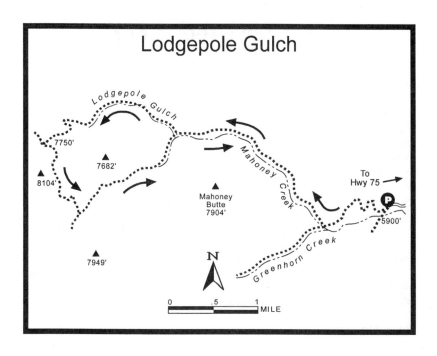

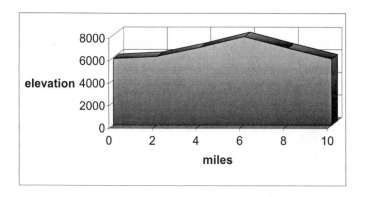

18. Cow Creek Loop

Length: 8.4 miles
Difficulty Rating: Moderate/Difficult
Technical Rating: 2+
The Ride: Loop
Starting Elevation: 5900'
High Point Elevation: 6900'
Total Elevation Gain: 1000'
Surface: Single track trail
Season: May - late October
Fun Factor: Wildflowers, climbing, great downhill, meadows.
Summary: This whole area is a great place for riding, no matter which loop you do. Cow Creek is still a bit of a primitive trail compared to the other trails in the area. Be prepared for a little bit of adventure.
Getting There: From Ketchum, drive south on Hwy 75 for 6 miles and turn west (right) at the light onto Greenhorn Gulch Road. Follow the road through Golden Eagle Subdivision to the end of the road, and follow the dirt road for half mile to the parking lot. The ride begins here.

Miles The Ride:

0.0 Follow the trail exiting the parking lot area on the west side. The beginning of this trail is quite rocky and rough, but don't let this turn you off.

1.0 Pass by Cow Creek Trail on the right. This is where you'll come out.

1.4 Trail junction: Turn right toward Mahoney Creek Trail and Lodgepole Trail and begin a gradual ascent.

3.7 You reach a trail junction. Turn right and into Lodgepole Gulch, and then after about 200 feet look right and follow a faint trail which begins to climb up and northeast. Be sure you're on the correct trail (2nd right), as there is an old trail just before the correct one. But remember, these are very faint. You'll follow this trail as it roller-coasters and contours along the hillsides to a nice big pond and boggy area.

5.4 The big pond and boggy area. At the far end of the wet area (east end), be sure to curve around to the south, by-passing a faint trail which peels off to the left and over a small saddle. That faint trail is a bit more adventurous as it gets lost in a log area before turning to serious boulder-hopping and the parking lot. Instead, stay on the trail heading south and down.

7.0 Trail junction: look familiar? That's right, you were here once before on your way out on the start. Turn left and head back up and over to the parking lot.

8.4 The parking lot and back at your car.

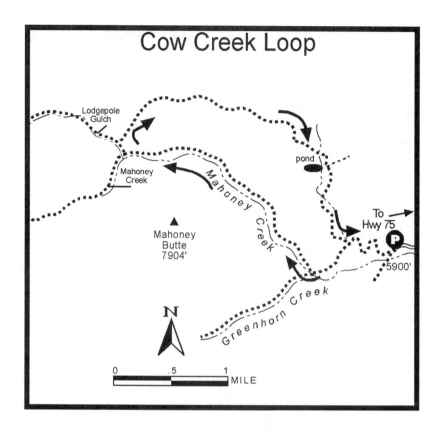

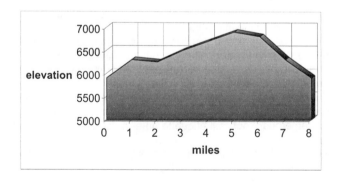

19. Greenhorn Gulch to Mahoney Creek

Length: 12.8 miles
Difficulty Rating: Difficult
Technical Rating: 2+
The Ride: Loop
Starting Elevation: 5900'
High Point Elevation: 8000'
Total Elevation Gain: 2100'
Surface: Single track trail
Season: May - late October
Fun Factor: Moderate climbs leading to excellent views and downhills.
Summary: This ride is always an aerobic challenge with wonderful single track trails, views of the Pioneer mountains and some of the best downhill riding around.
Getting There: From Ketchum, drive south on Hwy 75 for 6 miles and turn west (right) at the light onto Greenhorn Gulch Road. Follow the road through Golden Eagle Subdivision to the end of the road, and follow the dirt road for half mile to the parking lot. The ride begins here.

Miles The Ride:

0.0 Follow the trail exiting the parking lot area on the west side. The beginning of this trail is quite rocky and rough, but don't let this turn you off.

1.0 Pass by Cow Creek Trail on the right.

1.4 Trail junction: Right trail leads to Mahoney Creek and Lodgepole Creek, but turn left and continue up toward "Deer Creek," ascending the trail through pines next to a stream.

3.8 An unsigned trail on the right leads up Mahoney Creek, continue straight on the main trail heading toward Deer Creek.

4.9 Catch your breath at the trail junction midway through the climb. Hard left eventually leads to Imperial Gulch Trail #155, while a soft left leads down a jeep trail to Deer Creek via Panther Creek. Instead, continue grinding up and right on Mahoney Creek Trail #156 climbing a few switchbacks eventually gaining the top of the ride with incredible views of the Pioneer mountains to the east.

6.6 After a few roller-coasters, you come to a trail junction. Left trail leads down Red Warrior Creek Trail #152, but continue down right on the main trail eventually passing by the unsigned Mahoney Creek trail in a saddle on the right side after 0.5 miles.

7.6 Trail junction: Left trail leads into Lodgepole Creek. Instead, continue down and right on the main trail through a wonderful tree slalom course. Please remember your trail etiquette here, no skidding and yield to all others.

9.1 Trail junction: Left trail leads up Lodgepole Creek. Continue the ride down on the main trail. Watch that smile, you may have to pick a few bugs out of your teeth.

11.4 The loop is complete. Continue left and down crossing the stream two more times, the same way you came up.

12.8 End of the ride at the parking lot.

Greenhorn Gulch to Mahoney

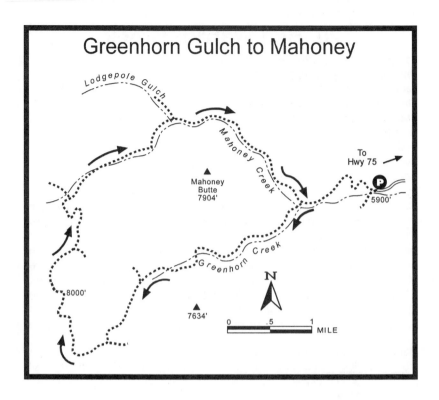

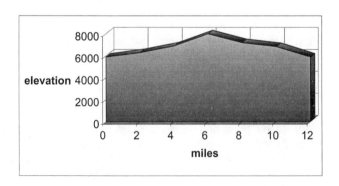

(This trail is sponsored by Formula Sports)

20. Red Warrior Creek

Length: 10.7 miles (30.2 miles for Loop)
Difficulty Rating: Difficult
Technical Rating: 3+
The Ride: One-way or loop option
Starting Elevation: 5900'
High Point Elevation: 7850'
Total Elevation Gain: 1950'
Surface: Single track trail and dirt jeep road
Season: May - late October
Fun Factor: Great climbing, killer descent and hot springs.
Summary: A ride up Lodgepole Gulch leads to a great technical descent through creeks and rocks to a huge creek crossing and hot springs. Views abound in every direction.
Getting There: From Ketchum, drive south on Hwy 75 for 6 miles and turn west (right) onto Greenhorn Gulch Road. There may be a stop light here soon. Drive 3.8 miles up the road to the parking lot. The ride begins here. **You may want to shuttle a car up Warm Springs Road to the end of the ride at Warfield Hot Springs, or plan on enjoying the casual ride back down Warm Springs Road into Ketchum and back to the trailhead (approx. 20 miles).

Miles	The Ride:
0.0	Follow the trail exiting the parking lot area on the west side. The trail is quite rocky and rough, but don't let this turn you off, it becomes great at the top.
1.0	Pass by Cow Creek Trail on the right.
1.4	Trail junction: Turn right toward Mahoney Creek Trail and Lodge poleTrail and begin a gradual ascent.
3.7	You reach a trail junction. Turn right and into Lodgepole Gulch. From here you climb about 1000' feet over the next 2.1 miles. It is never too hard, so take many deep breaths, endure the grind and relax and enjoy the beautiful scenes.
5.8	At the next trail junction, turn right heading up and over into RedWarrior Creek. The left fork here drops down into Mahoney Creek.
6.1	At the saddle between Lodgepole Gulch and Red Warrior Creek, youbegin some fast descending switchbacks for the next 1.2 miles. Once at the bottom and into the Red Warrior Creek drainage, pre pare to get wet. You'll cross the creek anywhere between 16 and 24 times, depending upon the time of year and dryness of the upper creek.
8.3	Continuing forward, you'll pass by a trail leading up and to the left. That trail eventually joins up to Mars Ridge.
9.2	Prepare for a gnarly descent. Soon you'll notice an old metal shack and from here the trail crosses the creek 8 times while the trail winds its way down the drainage.

10.7   The climax of the ride . . . crossing over Warm Springs Creek. No, there is not a bridge, so get wet and enjoy it. This is the end of the ride if you shuttled a car to this point. Warm Springs Road is right in front of you, as are about three hot-springs next to the creek a couple hundred yards down the road. Turn right, and from here it is approximately ten miles back to Ketchum, and an additional ten miles back to the Greenhorn Gulch Trailhead, all gradually descending.

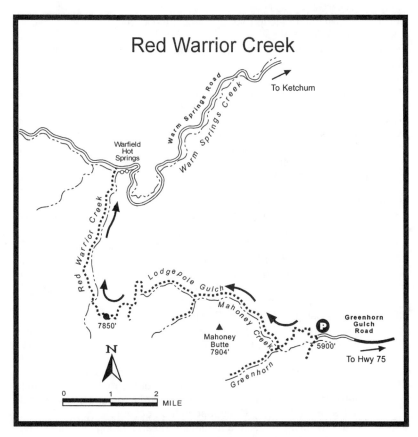

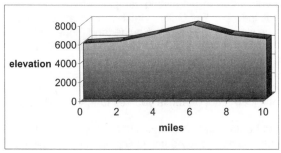

21. Eve Gulch

Length: 14.5 miles
Difficulty Rating: Abusive
Technical Rating: 3+
The Ride: Loop
Starting Elevation: 5600'
High Point Elevation: 7900'
Total Elevation Gain: 2300'
Surface: Pavement, dirt jeep road and single track trail
Season: May - late October
Fun Factor: Incredible views of three mountain ranges, wildlife, wildflowers.
Summary: This is certainly not a first date ride. However, if you are an abusive rider, then this ride has your name all over it. Endless steep climbing and rocky downhills will be your entertainment.
Getting There: From Ketchum, drive north on Hwy 75 for 3 blocks and turn left at the light and onto Warm Springs Road. Drive 1/2 mile further to the corner of Warm Springs Road and Saddle Road. Park in the parking lot of the Park & Ride lot (big vacant lot) on the east side (right side) of the road to begin the ride, or park anywhere close by.

Miles	The Ride:
0.0	Begin by crossing the bridge over the Big Wood River and riding westup Warm Springs Road. Be careful, this is a busy road.
1.6	Four way stop sign. Continue forward and up the main road.
3.0	Pass Penny Lake on the left side of the road.
5.7	Whoa! Turn right here at the West Fork Warm Springs Creek (Eve Gulch) trail #146. This is where the fun begins and the climbing stops . . . or is it the other way around?
6.8	After passing by Moonlight Gulch, take the right fork.
7.3	The road takes a sharp right turn and starts a grueling climb up the sideof the mountain, continually steep at times. Hey, good for the heart, huh?
8.0	After the road makes a sharp left on a switchback onto the ridge, look for a small cairn off to the right side of the road leading to the single-track trail after about a hundred yards (note: the single track trail is before the very steep road in front of you).
8.6	After traversing across the mountainside and through the pinetrees, you encounter an old mining camp.
8.8	At last, the top of Eve Gulch. Catch your breath and check out the 360 degree views of the Smoky, Boulder and Pioneer Mountains. Follow the trail to the right and down into Eve Gulch. Be careful here, the trail can be quite rutted and loose at times.
10.0	The single-track becomes a double-track jeep trail.
11.0	Junction with Adams Gulch Road #141. Turn right here and continue down the jeep road, or abuse yourself further and do the Adams Gulch Loop.
11.4	Turn right onto Shadyside Trail #177A, a single-track trail which contours the hillside above Adams Gulch on the south side of the canyon.

12.9 At the end of Shadyside Trail, turn right and up the hill on the rather wide trail known as "Heidelberg Hill." After gaining the saddle a short distance later, continue down the drainage either on the jeep trail or the single-track on the left side. No more climbing, we promise.

13.7 End of the dirt trail and the beginning of the pavement. Turn left here on Hillside then an immediate right onto Wanderer. At the intersection with Warm Springs Road, turn left and continue back to your car at the Park-n-Ride lot area.

14.5 End of the ride and back at your car. Whew! Where's the PowerTarts?!

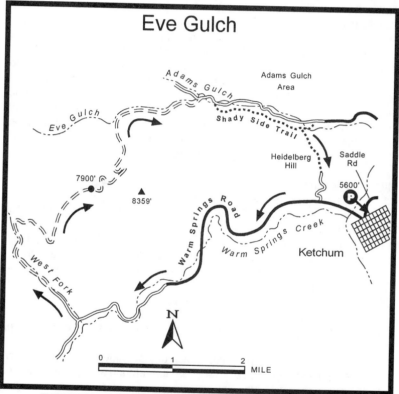

Eve Gulch

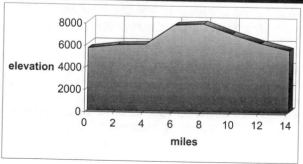

22. Corral Creek

Length: 6.8 miles
Difficulty: Easy/Moderate
Technical Rating: 1
The Ride: Out & Back
Starting Elevation: 6075'
High Point: 6750'
Total Elevation Gain: 675'
Ride Surface: Single track trail
Riding Season: Late April - late October
Fun Factor: Sagebrush slalom courses with incredible downhills.
Summary: This ride has it all, quick climbs (never too steep), quick turns in a slalom fashion, and one of the best downhills this close to Ketchum.
Getting There: From Ketchum, drive east on Sun Valley/Trail Creek Road for 3.7 miles, passing by Trail Creek Cabin along the way. Turn right where the sign points to Trail Creek Trailhead, just past the Boundary Campground. Besure to park in the trailhead parking lot and NOT the picnic or campground areas. The ride begins here. (*please note that this is a new trailhead starting late-summer 2003, the old trailhead was located behind Trail Creek Cabin. Please do not use the old trailhead.)

Miles	The Ride:
0.0	Begin by riding down the gravel trail through the campground and across the bridge. Follow this trail up the embankment to the trail junction.
0.1	Trail junction. Turn left and follow the single track trail along the foothills heading up the valley. Remember to stay on single track the entire time, since you will be crossing a few faint jeep roads along the way.
1.4	Whoa! Trail junction. Stay to the right on the main trail. The left fork leads down to Trail Creek Road.
2.9	Junction with a jeep road crossing. Simply cross the road and keep cruising!
3.4	Take a minute, unpack your lunch or just enjoy Uncle Johns Gulch and the sheep corrals. From here turn around and get ready for the best ride of your life.
6.8	End of the ride and return to Trail Creek Trailhead parking lot.

(This trail is sponsored by Jytte Mau Designs)

"Your actions are simulaneously the result of past karma and the creation of new karma. Action creates memory, and memory creates desire. Desire produces further action, which continues the cycle of karma. To be aware of this reality and to master your actions are the keys to creating the karma of happiness."

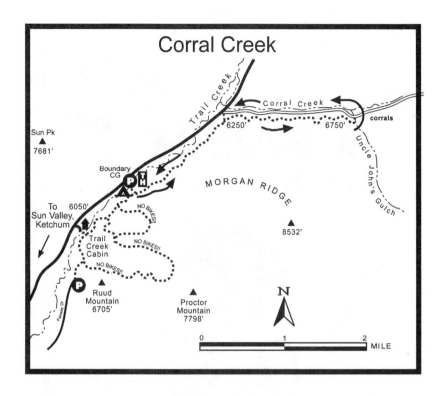

Corral Creek

Sun Pk
▲
7681'

Trail Creek

Corral Creek

corrals

6250'

6750'

Uncle John's Gulch

Boundary CG

MORGAN RIDGE

To Sun Valley, Ketchum

6050'

NO BIKES!!

NO BIKES!!

NO BIKES!!

Trail Creek Cabin

▲
8532'

Fairway Dr

Ruud Mountain
6705'

Proctor Mountain
7798'

N

0   1   2
MILE

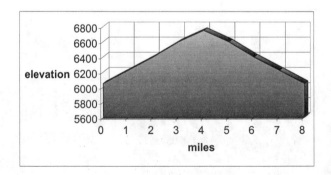

elevation

23. Placer Creek to Castle Creek

Length: 10.9 miles
Difficulty Rating: Moderate/Difficult
Technical Rating: 3+
The Ride: Loop
Starting Elevation: 6640'
High Point Elevation: 8220'
Total Elevation Gain: 1580'
Surface: Dirt jeep road and single track
Season: Late May to October
Fun Factor: Adventure and the feeling of being way out there.
Summary: If you can get by the loose rock and pushing for a little ways on the way up, you'll dig the downhill all the way back to your car.
Getting There: From Ketchum, drive north on Hwy 75 for 3 blocks and turn left at the light and onto Warm Springs Road. Follow this road for approximately 15.5 miles and park on the left just after the trailhead sign for Castle Creek. You'll know you're there when a big castle-like rock appears on the north side of the creek. This is where the ride begins.

<u>Miles</u>	<u>The Ride</u>:
0.0	Begin by riding up Warm Springs Road to the turn off for Placer Creek.
1.3	Turn right on the jeep road next to the corrals. Stay on this main road.
2.3	Cross the obvious creek in front of you.
3.0	Another creek crossing . . . enjoy the wetness!
3.1	This rough road leads to a small sign on the right. Follow the trail to the right.
4.8	Stay on the main trail here.
5.0	The trail starts to level out a bit and then hits a very marshy area. It's not that bad, and the upper end of the water crested stream has some small logs to cross on. From here follow the trail through the forest where it goes through numerous springs and over logs. Eventually it dries out.
5.5	The top of the ride. Get ready for the most amazing downhill. Be careful!
6.6	After some serious switchbacks, you cross over Castle Creek. Go right.
8.3	Cross over the North Fork of Castle Creek. Look upstream for a crossing.
9.5	The trail goes through a huge meadow and disappears. Stay straight through the meadow and the trail reappears at the other end.
10.7	Cross through Castle Creek. Get wet, you're almost done!
10.8	Cross through Warm Springs Creek. Keep trying until you get it. Get wet!
10.9	After crossing Warm Springs Creek, turn right on the road and to your car.

"Your behavior while people are watching is important. However, your behavior while no one is watching is more important, for it reveals your true character."

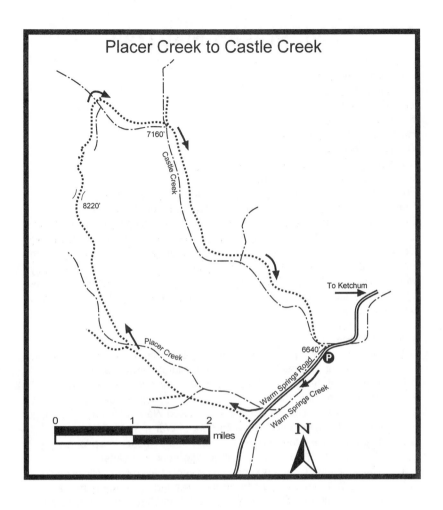

Placer Creek to Castle Creek

7160'

Castle Creek

8220'

To Ketchum

Placer Creek

6640'

Warm Springs Road

P

Warm Springs Creek

0   1   2 miles

N

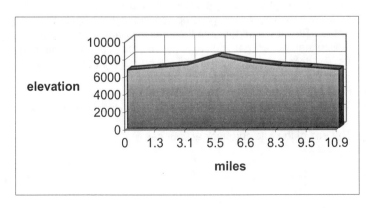

elevation

10000
8000
6000
4000
2000
0

0   1.3   3.1   5.5   6.6   8.3   9.5   10.9

miles

24. Poison Flat Trail

Length: 13.2 miles
Difficulty Rating: Difficult
Technical Rating: 2+
The Ride: One-way
Starting Elevation: 6850'
High Point Elevation: 7900'
Total Elevation Gain: 1050'
Surface: Dirt jeep road and single track trail
Season: Late May - late October
Fun Factor: Wildflowers, high alpine meadows, cruiser downhills.
Summary: Moderate climbing, great views and incredible downhills
Getting There: From the heart of Ketchum, drive north on Hwy 75 for 3 blocks and turn left onto Warm Springs Road. Follow this road up Warm Springs Canyon approximately 18 miles where a pull-out on the left shows signs for Road #046 (South and Middle Forks of Warm Springs Creek). Park anywhere near here. You will need to shuttle a car to the North Fork of Deer Creek parking area (see the North Fork of Deer Creek ride #12 on page 38 for directions).

Miles The Ride:

0.0   Begin by riding up the South Fork of Warm Springs #046 in a southerly direction on a partial jeep road, immediately forging a stream.

0.7   Turn left at the sign for Meadow Creek Trail and cross the creek.

1.0   Again, turn left at the sign for South Fork of Warm Springs Trail #151.

2.4   Trail junction: The left fork goes up to Red Warrior Creek. Instead, go right and continue up the South Fork of Warm Springs Trail #199.

3.1   The trail turns into a tough climb up through loose scree for only a short distance, gaining a small saddle soon thereafter.

4.3   Trail junction: Do not go right, it is a very challenging trail which could involve a few tears and hair pulling. Instead, save the marriage and turn left onto the Poison Flat Trail #218 and begin a scenic cruise across the high alpine sage-brush meadow.

6.6   Trail junction: The left fork goes up and over into the North Fork of Deer Creek. Take the right fork into the main drainage of Deer Creek. However, either trail will get you back to your (shuttled) car at the trailhead.

8.7   As you descend, pass by Horn Creek on the right and a mile later is Bear Gulch.

10.7 Pass by Curran Gulch on the right side.

12.0 The trailhead for Deer Creek Trail and a primitive hunters camp. Continue on down the main jeep road.

13.2 The end of the ride and back at your car.

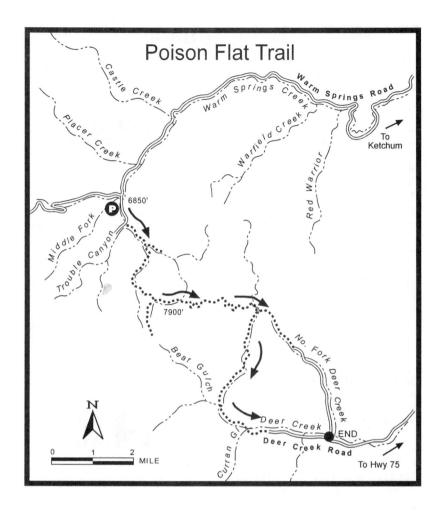

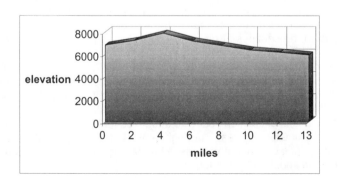

25. The Bald Mountain Trails

Warm Springs Trail
Length: 9.1 miles
Difficulty Rating: Moderate
Technical Rating: 1
The Ride: One-way
Starting Elevation: 9010'
Ending Elevation: 5880'
Total Elevation Gain/Loss: 3130'
Surface: Single track trail
Season: May - October

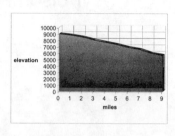

Fun Factor: Views, incredible views and more views.
Summary: If you're riding up the trail, it gradually climbs and switchbacks most of the way up this side of the mountain before gaining a ridge and winding its way to the top via the west side of the mountain. If you're riding down, be cautious of other riders and hikers moving in your opposite direction.
Trailhead Directions: From Ketchum Main Street, drive north turning left at the light leading to Warm Springs Road. Follow this road as it winds through a Ketchum business district and over the Big Wood River. Approximately 2 miles from Ketchum, at the four way stop sign, turn left leading to the base of Warm Springs side of Bald Mountain. The trailhead is located at the base of the ski run, next to the lodge.

Cold Springs Trail
Length: 8.6 miles
Difficulty Rating: Moderate
Technical Rating: 2
The Ride: One-way
Starting Elevation: 9010'
Ending Elevation: 5680'
Total Elevation Gain/Loss: 3330'
Surface: Single track trail
Season: May - October
Fun Factor: Views, incredible views and more views.
Summary: If you're riding up this side of the mountain, it is rather steep until you reach the Cold Springs chairlift. From here it's gradual cruising up and around the south side of the mountain, eventually reaching the top. If you're riding down, be cautious of other riders and hikers moving in your opposite direction.
Trailhead Directions: From the Main Street (Hwy 75) and Sun Valley Road stop light in Ketchum, go west on Third Street heading toward the mountain. After four blocks the road takes a natural left and becomes Third Avenue. Follow this road as it winds its way to the River Run base of the mountain. Park here and backtrack on your bike about 100 feet to the bike path and ride south approximately 2 miles. Turn right at the trailhead sign and begin riding up Cold Springs canyon. If you passed under the highway on the bike path, you've gone about 100 yards too far.

Lower River Run Trail

Length: 9 miles
Difficulty Rating: Moderate
Technical Rating: 1+
The Ride: One-way
Starting Elevation: 5680'
High Point Elevation: 7350"
Total Elevation Gain: 1670'
Surface: Single track trail
Season: May - October

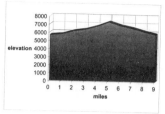

Fun Factor: Views, incredible views and more views.

Summary: This is a great post-work, quick ride that'll get you from one side of Bald Mountain to the other. It is also great access to the top of the mountain. There are maps the entire way, so you'll have to seriously try hard to get lost.

Trailhead Directions: From the Main Street (Hwy 75) and Sun Valley Road stop light in Ketchum, go west on Third Street heading toward the mountain. After four blocks the road takes a natural left and becomes Third Avenue. Follow this road as it winds its way to the River Run base of the mountain. Park anywhere near the ski lifts. Mount up and ride over the bridge between the two large buildings and veer right of the ski lift and look for the trailhead taking off left under the lift. It is 5 miles of casual climbing before the descent into Warm Springs. From there, take the roads back into town and back to the River Run side of Bald Mountain and your car.

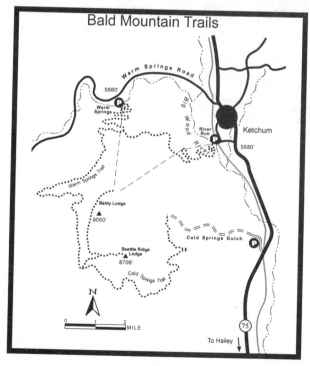

Get your stickers at local shops and help support our trails!

26. Adams Gulch Area Rides

Adams Gulch is a heavily used area due to its close proximity to Ketchum. The trails here are used by hikers, trail runners, mountain bikers and equestrians. Please be considerate of others using the trails and stay in complete control while descending. Ride mileages may vary depending where you start from. Some mileages are listed as "one-way" which doesn't mean it is rideable only in one direction, but rather the mileage is only from one end of the ride to the other.

Getting There: From Ketchum, drive north on Hwy 75 for 1.5 miles and turn left at the sign for Adams Gulch Road. Follow this road down and through the subdivision, crossing over the river and veering right. Approximately 1/4 mile later at the T-intersection, turn left and up the road, gaining the trailhead and parking area about 1 mile later.

Adams Gulch Loop

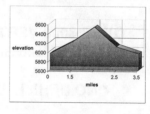

Length: 7 miles
Difficulty Rating: Difficult
Technical Rating: 2+
The Ride: loop
Starting Elevation: 5950'
High Point Elevation: 7220'
Total Elevation Gain: 1270'
Surface: Dirt jeep road and single track trail
Season: Late May - October
Fun Factor: The ultimate loop complete with the complimentary grind.
Summary: Typically a clock-wise ride, you get a great warm-up on the jeep road before hitting the single track which is a constant grind to the top with periodic rests. Once topped out, the downhill is nothing short of spectacular. Well worth the work!

(This trail is sponsored by Backwoods Mtn Sports & Sun Summit Ski & Cycle)

Lane's / Sunnyside Trails

Length: 3.5 miles
Difficulty Rating: Easy/Moderate
Technical Rating: 1+
The Ride: Loop
Starting Elevation: 5950'
High Point Elevation: 6520'
Total Elevation Gain: 570'
Surface: Dirt jeep road and single track trail
Season: May - October
Fun Factor: Picnic table rest at the top with phenomenal views.
Summary: While Shadyside is obviously in the shade, this one is directly opposite. You want sun? Come and get it! We like riding this one clock-wise, due to the gradual warm-up on the jeep road. Once it hits the single track, you grind for a bit before backing off and topping out at a picnic table. From here the descent is fun, fast and furious. *(This trail is sponsored by The Elephants Perch)*

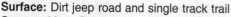

Shadyside Trail

Length: 3 miles
Difficulty Rating: Easy/Moderate
Technical Rating: 1+
The Ride: Loop
Starting Elevation: 5950'
High Point Elevation: 6200'
Total Elevation Gain: 250'

Surface: Dirt jeep road and single track trail

Season: Late May - October

Fun Factor: A definite fun warm up on a hot summer day.

Summary: This ride is never too technical or hard, aside from the start, which is not an indicator for the rest of the ride.

(This trail is sponsored by Sturtevants Ski & Sports-Sturtos)

Adams Gulch Trail

Length: 14 miles
Difficulty Rating: Abusive
Technical Rating: 4
The Ride: Loop
Starting Elevation: 5950'
High Point Elevation: 8400'
Total Elevation Gain: 2450'

Surface: Dirt jeep road and single track trail

Season: Late May - October

Fun Factor: This ride defines the word fun. Hills, views and downhills.

Summary: This is a serious ride. It seems longer than it is due to its technical nature. Have the right attitude from the onset or don't go.

Harpers Trail

Length: 3.5 miles
Difficulty Rating: Moderate
Technical Rating: 2
The Ride: Loop
Starting Elevation: 5950'
High Point Elevation: 7000'
Total Elevation Gain: 1050'

Surface: Single track trail

Season: Late May - October

Fun Factor: Another great loop which connects Fox Creek and Lake Creek into the Adams Gulch Area.

Summary: Great in either direction, but we personally like this one counterclockwise. A short grind leads to rollers into Lake Creek area before gradual grinding up to the top where you encounter the Adams Gulch Loop descent.

(This trail is sponsored by the SVSEF with Fox Creek Linkage sponsored by Chateau Drug)

70

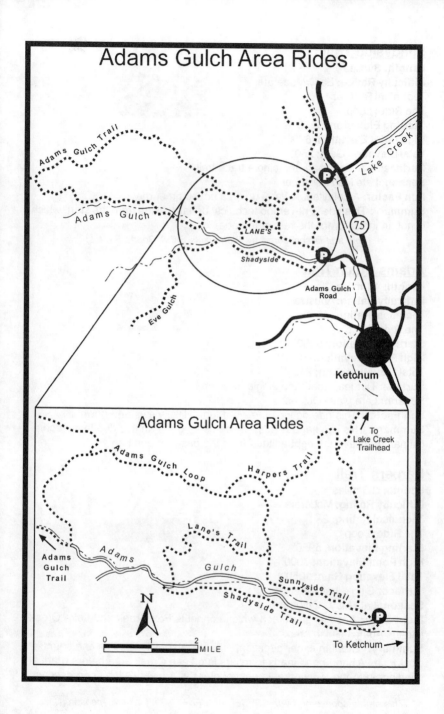

Adams Gulch Loop and Ketchum in the Background- McBob Collection

www.royalrobbins.com

27. Fox Creek

Length: 6.6 miles
Difficulty Rating: Moderate
Technical Rating: 1+
The Ride: Loop
Starting Elevation: 5950'
High Point Elevation: 6700'
Total Elevation Gain: 750'
Surface: Single track trail and dirt jeep road.
Season: Late May - October
Fun Factor: Moderate climbs, great descents, and wildflowers.
Summary: This is undoubtedly one of the best all-around rides close to Ketchum. Never too steep to ride and always a good time on the downhills.
Getting There: From Ketchum, drive north on Highway 75 for 4 miles to the Lake Creek Trailhead and turn left into the parking lot. The ride begins here. (**Access to the Lake Creek Trailhead may be hindered by flood waters in early season. If this is the case, turn around and drive back 0.5 miles on the highway to Hulen Meadows Road and turn right. Follow the road across the bridge, and park on the right immediately in the gravel parking area. Ride up the road staying right until the cul-de-sac. Follow the trail next to the driveway heading north at the end of the cul-de-sac. In 1/4 mile you join up with the main Lake Creek trail coming in from the right. For Summer 2004 there will be a new trailhead located approx. 7 miles north of Ketchum.

Miles The Ride:

0.0 From the Lake Creek trailhead parking lot, ride across the steel bridge and the Big Wood River. Follow this trail as it winds to the right through the trees and next to the river.

0.2 Ride up a small embankment to where it intersects with a jeep road. Turn right here.

0.6 Trail junction: The left fork here is where the Fox Creek Loop comes out. Stay straight on the jeep trail heading north.

1.3 The jeep road turns to single track and quickly comes to a shale/rock traverse. After roller-coastering along, you will cross two small bridges.

1.9 An intensely steep switchback leads up and away from the river, fol lowed by a similarly steep downhill and a quick slalom course through the aspen trees.

2.4 Cross over Fox Creek and come to a trail junction: Turn left here on the Fox Creek Trail. The right fork will put you on the North Fork Trail.

2.6 Another trail junction: Take the left (straight) fork to continue heading up stream into Fox Creek. The right fork leads into the upper section of the North Fork Loop.

3.1 After crossing over two bridges, you reach another trail junction. Stay on the left (straight) fork heading upstream into Fox Creek. The right fork leads to Oregon Gulch and/or Chocolate Gulch. From here the trail becomes a "one-way" only trail for mountain bikers. Be cautious here, runners and hikers could be coming in the other direction. After a couple 100 yards cross over Fox Creek and begin a gradual climb up switchbacks.

4.1   Come to a saddle and continue on. The faint trail off to the right of the trail here leads to a nice bench in the meadow.

6.0   Join the main trail again as the loop is now complete. Turn right and continue back to the trail head at Lake Creek or Hulen Meadows.

6.6   End of the ride and back at your car.

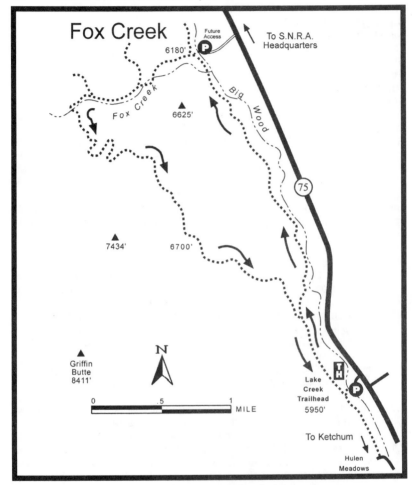

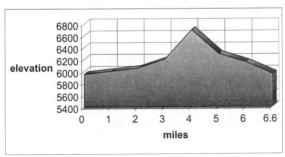

28. Chocolate Gulch

Length: 3.8 miles
Difficulty Rating: Moderate/Difficult
Technical Rating: 2+
The Ride: Loop
Starting Elevation: 6150'
High Point Elevation: 6750'
Total Elevation Gain: 600'
Surface: Single track trail
Season: Mid-May - late October
Fun Factor: Moderate climbing to incredible views of the Wood River Valley.
Summary: This is a rather short but fun ride that has moderate climbing, creek crossings, technical rock moves, views and a great descent. On top of that, it has access to three other rides in the immediate surrounding area.
Getting There: From Ketchum, drive north on Highway 75 approximately 6.8 miles and turn left on Chocolate Gulch Road (just after crossing over the Big Wood River). Drive to the end of the road and park here. This parking area can usually get crowded so please respect the private property and only park in the designated area. If it is too crowded in the parking area please choose another ride or park at the Oregon Gulch parking area just north about 1/2 mile. For Summer 2004 there will be a new trailhead located approx. 7 miles north of Ketchum.

Miles The Ride:

0.0 From the parking area ride west and immediately onto the single track which takes a quick switchback to the left and gradually climbs a bit to the Chocolate Gulch trail #149B. Turn right here.

0.3 After crossing a small bridge, a muddy bog and the stream, take a sharp left around the willows and start a gradual climb, passing by the right fork for Saddle Trail which leads over the hills to Oregon Gulch (1.9 mi. long).

0.6 Forge another stream crossing leading to moderate climbing.

1.5 Top of the first saddle. This is a false summit, keep going, almost there!

1.7 Top of the second saddle and the high-point of the ride. Continue on down the trail passing by a difficult rock/sand/scree pile and into a couple of switchbacks. Be careful here, the trail could be fairly loose.

2.1 Junction. The left fork is the continuation of the Chocolate Gulch trail, while the right fork is the Oregon Gulch/Fox Creek Loop #149C. Make a left turn here.

2.4 Junction. The left fork is the continuation of the Chocolate Gulch trail along with Fox Creek Loop (you are now on one trail of two different names). Don't get confused, just look at the sign. Go left here. Taking the right trail would lead to the upper section of Fox Creek.

2.7 After a few roller-coasters, you cross over Fox Creek on two bridges.

2.9 Junction. Take the left fork here on the North Fork Loop #149A and start climbing up a switchback. It seems steep but is relatively short.

3.5 Junction with the lower section of the North Fork Loop. Continue straight.

3.8 End of the ride and back at the trailhead.

(This trail is sponsored by Premier Resorts)

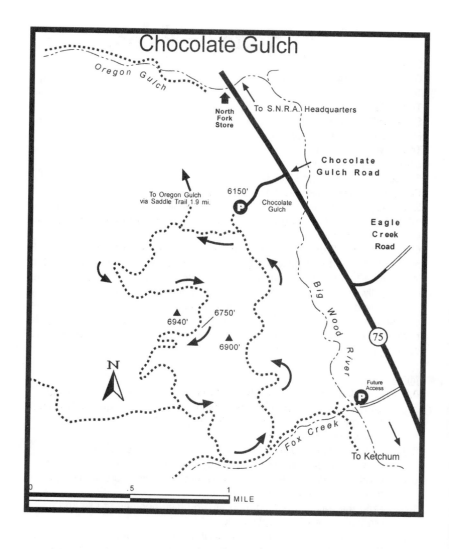

Chocolate Gulch

Oregon Gulch

To S.N.R.A. Headquarters

North Fork Store

Chocolate Gulch Road

To Oregon Gulch via Saddle Trail 1.9 mi.

6150'

P

Chocolate Gulch

Eagle Creek Road

▲ 6940'

6750'

▲ 6900'

N

Big Wood River

75

Future Access

P

Fox Creek

To Ketchum

0   .5   1   MILE

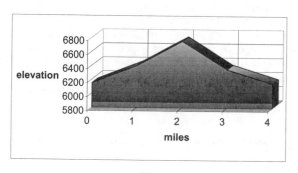

elevation

6800
6600
6400
6200
6000
5800

0   1   2   3   4

miles

29. North Fork Loop

Length: 2.6 miles
Difficulty Rating: Moderate
Technical Rating: 2+
The Ride: Loop
Starting Elevation: 6150'
High Point Elevation: 6350'
Total Elevation Gain: 200'
Surface: Single track trail
Season: Early May - late October
Fun Factor: Quick, technical, views and river.
Summary: The North Fork Loop is usually considered as a starting point for other rides. However, the loop in itself is a great warm-up for Chocolate Gulch or Fox Creek.
Getting There: From Ketchum, drive north on Highway 75 approximately 6.8 miles and turn left on Chocolate Gulch Road (just after crossing over the Big Wood River). Drive to the end of the road and park here. This parking area can usually get a bit crowded so please respect the private property and only park in the designated area. If it is too crowded in the parking area please choose another ride or park in the Oregon Gulch parking area about half mile north on the highway. For Summer 2004 there will be a new trailhead located approx. 7 miles north of Ketchum.

Miles <u>**The Ride:**</u>

0.0   From the parking area ride west and immediately onto the single track which takes a quick switchback to the left and gradually climbs a bit passing the Chocolate Gulch trail #149B on the right. Stay straight on the main trail here.

0.3   Junction with the North Fork Loop trail #149A. Go right here. From here be careful as the trail crosses over a steep hillside and rocks.

0.4   Gain a small saddle then immediately drop into a creek and imme diately climb a short hill.

1.0   After the trail roller-coasters a bit, you gain another saddle and be gin the descent into Fox Creek.

1.3   Junction with Fox Creek. The North Fork Loop goes to the left here. If you want to combine any other ride in the area, going right would lead to Chocolate Gulch, Fox Creek or Oregon Gulch.

1.5   Junction. The left fork leads on into the rest of the North Fork Loop. The right fork leads to the Lake Creek trailhead and Fox Creek.

2.1   Skinny bridge, be careful here especially when it is wet.

2.3   A steep pitch leads back to the beginning of the loop. Turn right at the top, continuing on the same trail.

2.6   After passing back by the Chocolate Gulch trailhead you find your self back at the car and the end of the ride.

"Your hopes and dreams are far more valid than your doubts and fears."

North Fork Loop

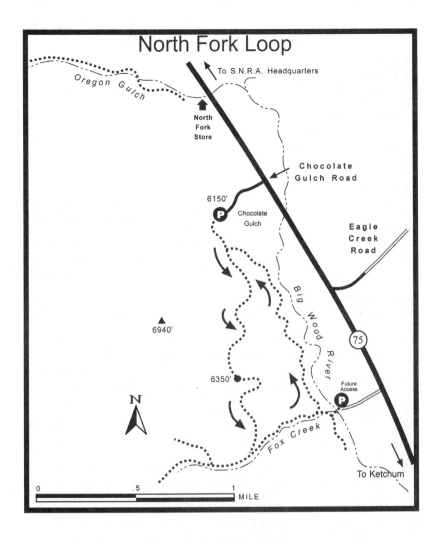

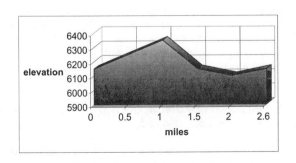

elevation

30. Oregon Gulch

Length: 11.0 miles
Difficulty Rating: Difficult
Technical Rating: 2+
The Ride: Loop
Starting Elevation: 6250'
High Point Elevation: 7600'
Total Elevation Gain: 2310'
Surface: Single track trail
Season: June through October
Fun Factor: Climbs, long downhills, streams, wildflowers.
Summary: This is one of those rides that is such a great time, you forget about the technical part instantly. Rock outcrops will test your balance and downhills will test your nerves.
Getting There: From Ketchum, drive north on Highway 75 for just over 7 miles to the North Fork Store. Turn left on the dirt road just past the store and behind the trailers. Follow this back to a grassy meadow with bathrooms. Park here.

Miles	The Ride:
0.0	Begin by riding up the single track trail on the west side of the parking area.
0.2	After entering into the trees you will encounter a junction with a trail leading over Saddle Trail (1.9 miles long) on the left and eventually into Chocolate Gulch. Instead, stay straight on the main trail which quickly goes down and over the creek where the trail continues up the gulch on the north side of the creek. This is Oregon Gulch.
1.3	Cross through the gate (please close it behind you).
3.2	Trail junction: Turn left here and cross the creek heading toward Fox Creek. The right fork goes up and eventually into the East Fork of Baker Creek.
4.6	Saddle, watch for the sharp right turn in about 100 yards.
5.0	Climb to a saddle and turn left into the gulch. The more worn right fork just climbs to a small overlook. From here the trail becomes a technical steep downhill with loose dirt and rocks.
7.0	Trail junction: Turn right and continue on the Oregon/Fox Creek Loop #149C. The left fork climbs up and over into Chocolate Gulch on Trail #146B.
7.25	Trail junction: Turn left and head downstream with Fox Creek.
7.5	After a few roller-coasters, you cross over Fox Creek on two bridges.
7.7	Junction. Take the left fork here on the North Fork Loop #149A and start climbing up a switch-back to a saddle.
8.3	Pass by the junction with the lower section of the North Fork Loop.
8.6	Turn left at the sign leading to Chocolate Gulch.
8.9	Turn right at the sign leading to Saddle Trail.
10.8	Back at the junction with Oregon Gulch Trail. Turn right here.
11.0	End of the ride and back at your car.

(This trail sponsored by Biy Wood Backcountry Trails, Ketchum/SV Rotary, Williams Market & Adventure Press)

Oregon Gulch

To Galena, Stanley

75

Big Wood River

North Fork

Wood River Campground

North Fork Campground

Sawtooth National Recreation Area Headquarters

Oregon Gulch

Saddle Trail

6200'

North Fork Store

To Ketchum

Chocolate Gulch

7933'

To Chocolate Gulch

7420'

6220'

Fox Creek

N

0   .5   1
MILE

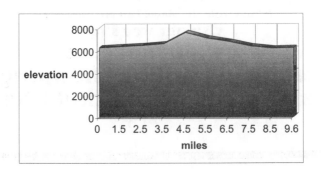

elevation

8000
6000
4000
2000
0

0   1.5   2.5   3.5   4.5   5.5   6.5   7.5   8.5   9.6

miles

31. Fox Peak

Length: 22.4 miles
Difficulty Rating: Abusive
Technical Rating: 4
The Ride: One-way
Starting Elevation: 6675'
High Point Elevation: 8720'
Total Elevation Gain: 2045'
Surface: Dirt jeep road to single track trail
Season: June - October
Fun Factor: Wicked downhills, climbs and traverses.
Summary: This is not a first date ride. Be ready for going over the front of your bike, falling and pushing.
Getting There: From Ketchum, drive north on Highway 75 approximately 15.5 miles and park on the right side of the road directly opposite of Baker Creek Road. The ride begins here.

<u>Miles</u> <u>The Ride</u>:

0.0 From the parking area, cross back over the highway and begin riding up Baker Creek Road #162.

3.1 Just after crossing over the East Fork of Baker Creek, turn left onto the East Fork of Baker Creek Road #68 and begin a gradual climb.

5.1 At the fork, take the lower (left), more traveled road which descends for a bit before climbing again.

5.7 When you come to the next fork, take the right (upper), more traveled road and begin climbing another pitch.

6.3 Encounter the switchbacks which are never too hard.

8.0 The saddle with a view. Continue on the jeep road passing by the trailhead to the Easley Loop around the next corner.

9.6 Pass by the Oregon Gulch access trailhead on the left.

9.7 Begin a fast descent on the jeep road, but keep a watch for a single-track turn-off in another 1.6 miles. It's easy to miss, unless you mean to.

11.3 Sign on the left says trail for Fox Creek and Adams Gulch. You can go this way if you want, but you'll have to push a bit. Instead, stay on the main road.

12.3 At the major intersection, stay left!

12.6 The double track dead ends at a berm. Single-track starts on the back side.

13.0 Trail junction: Stay left on Trail #142 to Adams Gulch.

14.0 Gain a small grassy saddle and begin a quick, exciting downhill.

14.2 Trail junction: The right fork leads into the top of Adams Gulch. Instead, stay straight on the main trail traversing the hillside. From here to the junction with Adams Gulch Loop, the trail is rocky, loose and intense in some places.

17.8 After climbing a short steep hill, the trail traverses down and into Adams Gulch.

19.3 Trail junction: You are now at the top of the Adams Gulch Loop Trail. Either direction (L or R) will take you down to the trailhead. But why not keep the fun rolling? Turn left.

20.2 Harpers Trail takes off to the left, but stay straight on Adams Gulch Loop.

22.4 The end of the ride and the parking area.

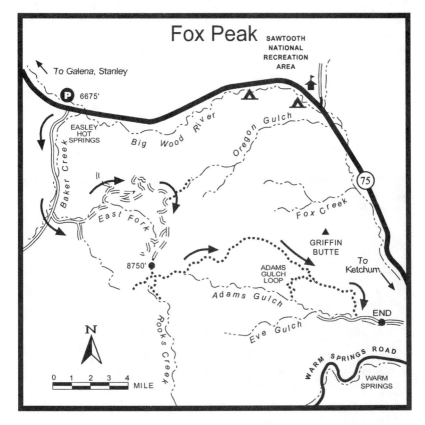

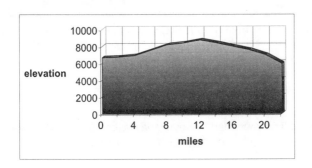

Riding in the Copper Basin Area

When you think of Copper Basin, the thoughts of dusty roads and mining tailings come to mind. Think again. We've only highlighted three rides in the area, one of which is currently closed, but there are a plethera of opportunities over there. Don't be afraid to be adventurous. The two open rides in this area, just happen to be two of our favorites, so take that for what it's worth.

While driving to this area, many cars have gotten flats from the sharp rocks on the roads. However, we have seen even the lowest sports cars driving on the roads. For an extra adventure after riding in the area, drive up and over Antelope Pass, which will take you towards Arco and Mackay areas. Enjoy some eats at Grandpa's BBQ in Arco, world famous!

Be adventurous and have some serious fun...go to Copper Basin!

Early mountain biking up Trail Creek outside Ketchum, circa 1945
Courtesy of Community Library, Ketchum, Idaho, Regional History Department

Write it on your heart that every day is the best day of the year.
— *Ralph Waldo Emerson*

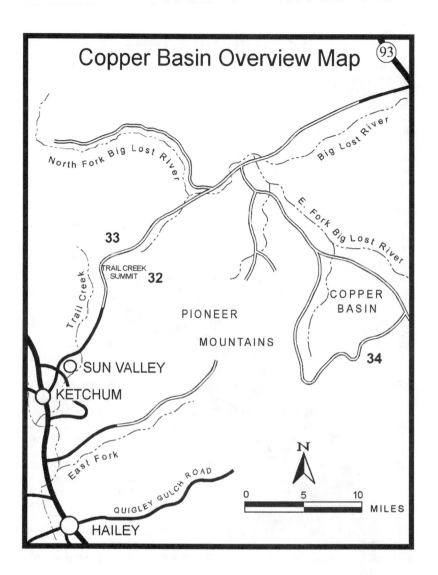

Copper Basin Overview Map

North Fork Big Lost River

Big Lost River

E. Fork Big Lost River

33

Trail Creek

TRAIL CREEK
SUMMIT 32

COPPER
BASIN

PIONEER

MOUNTAINS

34

SUN VALLEY

KETCHUM

East Fork

QUIGLEY GULCH ROAD

HAILEY

N

0   5   10

MILES

93

32. Summit Creek

Length: 19.5 miles
Difficulty Rating: Difficult
Technical Rating: 3 (descending off top)
The Ride: Loop
Starting Elevation: 7894'
High Point Elevation: 9480'
Total Elevation Gain: 1586' (2360' for entire loop)
Surface: Single track trail, dirt jeep road and gravel road
Season: June - September
Fun Factor: Incredible views of the Pioneer Mountains, wildlife and wild flowers.
Summary: With stunning views the entire time, you are given the climax right at the top of this pump-fest, oxygen-deprived ride with the Devils Bedstead.
Getting There: From the Main Street/Sun Valley Road intersection in Ketchum, drive east toward Sun Valley Resort. Continue on up the road, eventually turning into Trail Creek Road. After 12.5 miles you reach Trail Creek Summit. Park in the area on the right just over the summit and begin the ride here. If you are shuttling a car to do the one-way version of this ride, continue driving down the road approximately 7.5 miles to the Kane Creek Road. Park on the right.

<u>Miles</u> <u>The Ride</u>:

0.0 From the parking area, ride up through the parking area until the obvious trail is in front of you. Cross the creek and begin climbing up a rather steep but rideable switchback.

0.75 After the trail levels off a bit, you cruise through a sometimes wet meadow then cross Summit Creek again. From here the trail is a fun series of gradual climbs and beautiful meadows for about 3 miles.

3.0 The trail begins its famous 1 mile climbing section with steep pitches then some level stretches afterward. Hang in there, the view is well worth it!

4.0 The top of Summit Creek! Looking to the east, you'll see the Devils Bedstead looming over your head (11,051 ft). Now start by looking for the trail going down into Kane Creek off the top of the summit (left). The trail is not obvious, but if you continue down to your left into Kane Creek, you will find it. If you ride forward on the trail instead of left off the top you'll ride into a boulder field. Look for cairns and other obvious trail signs.

6.8 Junction with the Kane Creek trail. Go left and down to the parking area.

7.2 Kane Creek parking lot, ride down the obvious road toward Trail Creek Road. An option is to turn left in ~3.5 miles and take the shorter alternative route.

12.1 Junction with Trail Creek Road. If you parked here, crack a liquid refreshment and drive on back to Ketchum. If you only own 1 car like most of us and left it at the summit of Trail Creek Road, saddle up, take a left turn and huff it the 7.5 miles and 775 ft back up to your car.

19.5 The end of the ride.

**CLOSURES LIKE THIS CAN HAPPEN IF YOU DO NOT SIGN INTO THE TRAILHEADS. PLEASE SIGN IN ALWAYS!!!!!!

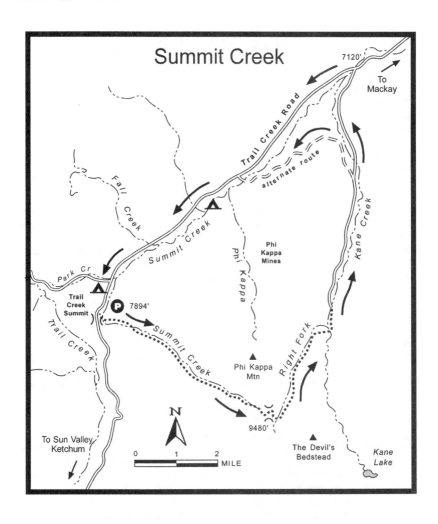

Summit Creek

7120'

To Mackay

Trail Creek Road

alternate route

Fall Creek

Summit Creek

Park Cr

Phi Kappa

Phi Kappa Mines

Kane Creek

Trail Creek Summit

7894'

Summit Creek

Phi Kappa Mtn

Right Fork

Trail Creek

N

To Sun Valley Ketchum

0   1   2   MILE

9480'

The Devil's Bedstead

Kane Lake

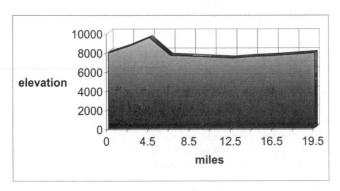

elevation

10000
8000
6000
4000
2000
0

0   4.5   8.5   12.5   16.5   19.5

miles

33. Park Creek

Length: 12.4 miles
Difficulty Rating: Moderate
Technical Rating: 2+
The Ride: Out and back
Starting Elevation: 7646'
High Point Elevation: 8500'
Total Elevation Gain: 854'
Surface: Dirt jeep road and single track trail
Season: Late May - October
Fun Factor: Gorgeous canyon, wildlife and trail finding.
Summary: Parker Creek is one of those hidden wonders in the Copper Basin area, where beautiful canyons, creeks, fishing and camping make for an entire weekend experience. The trail is a bit rough in places, but has recently been redone to make it a soon to be classic.
Getting There: From the Main Street/Sun Valley Road interection in Ketchum, drive east toward Sun Valley, passing the resort complex area and continue on up the road eventually becoming Trail Creek Road. After 12.5 miles you reach Trail Creek Summit. Continue on the main road for another 0.7 miles and park on the left at the junction of Park Creek Road #140 and Trail Creek. The ride begins here.

Miles The Ride:

0.0 Begin by riding up road #140 heading north and west through a large meadow.

1.2 Road to the left leads to the High Ridge Trail trailhead. Continue on Parker Creek Road up the canyon. For the next 1.5 miles you'll encounter many primitive campsites and meadows.

2.6 Road ends and single-track continues on.

2.7 Major stream crossing over Parker Creek.

3.9 Whoa! Look for the cairn on the right of the road to show you where to cross the creek (A little ways further the main road fades away into nothing). Instead, cross the creek, look for a faint trail leading uphill and into some trees. There you'll find a better trail leading left (north). This is not too difficult to find. Sounds difficult, but it snot.

4.3 A stream crossing leads to a series of springs and mud bogs.

4.7 Encounter another small meadow with bogs.

4.9 Whoa! After a steep crossing over a small creek, veer left on the other side of the creek following the contour of the creek and looking for the cairns.

5.0 Be sure to follow the trail heading left at all of the downed timber. From here the trail begins climbing up the canyon following the creek at all times.

5.4 The trail contours the creek at a very steep angle here.

6.2 At the edge of the completely downed forest in front of you is the end of the ride. After exploring further up the canyon from here, I'm convinced that a chainsaw is mandatory equipment, I just haven't found the proper bike mount...yet. Turn around and retrace your route. This ride could be an even better loop if someone had the will and power to do some logging.

12.4 The end of the ride and back at your car.

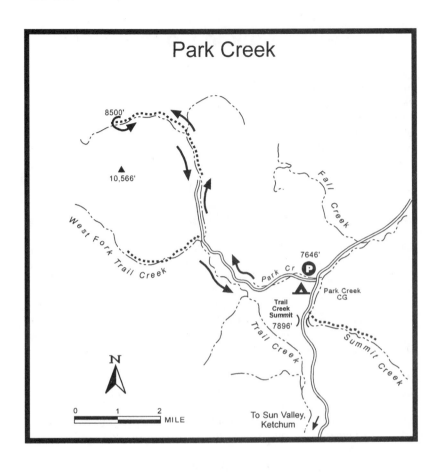

Park Creek

8500'

10,566'

West Fork Trail Creek

Fall Creek

7646'

Park Cr

Park Creek CG

Trail Creek Summit
7896'

Summit Creek

Trail Creek

N

0 1 2 MILE

To Sun Valley, Ketchum

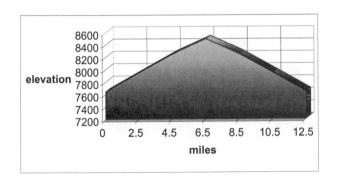

elevation

8600
8400
8200
8000
7800
7600
7400
7200

0   2.5   4.5   6.5   8.5   10.5   12.5

miles

34. Lake Creek in Copper Basin

Length: 13.8 miles
Difficulty Rating: Difficult
Technical Rating: 2+
The Ride: Loop
Starting Elevation: 8080'
High Point Elevation: 9650'
Total Elevation Gain: 1570'
Surface: Single track trail
Season: June - October
Fun Factor: The Pioneer Mountains, lakes and great fishing!
Summary: Truly one of the classics of Copper Basin. Put your fun-hat on and get ready for a great ride amidst lakes and the Pioneer Mountains.
Getting There: From the stop light in Ketchum, at the Main Street and Sun Valley Road intersection, drive east up Sun Valley Road heading toward Trail Creek Summit. After reaching the summit at 12.5 miles, drive 10.3 miles to Wildhorse/Copper Basin Road #135. Turn right and drive down the road 2 miles to the junction of Copper Basin Road and Wildhorse Creek Road. Turn left here and drive another 16 dusty miles (it's worth it), turning right at the second Copper Basin Loop Road sign. Cruise another 4.5 miles up the road to the Lake Creek turn-off. Park here, this is where the ride begins.

Miles The Ride:

0.0 Begin by riding up the trail, slowly winding your way up the valley, eventually getting to a rather large meadow.

3.9 At the fork near the cabin, turn left and get ready for a bit of a grind.

6.1 Catch your breath and pass by the trail over to Round Lake, the first of four lakes.

6.6 Cruise past Long Lake, or stop to cool off.

7.5 After a short steep pitch, you arrive at Rough Lake.

8.6 The final of four lakes, Big Lake, is reached after a short, gradual ascent.

9.8 Back at the original start of the lollipop loop. Turn left and continue back to the trailhead.

13.8 End of the ride and back at your car.

"When someone's character is not clear to you, look at that person's friends."
                                                            -Japanese Proverb

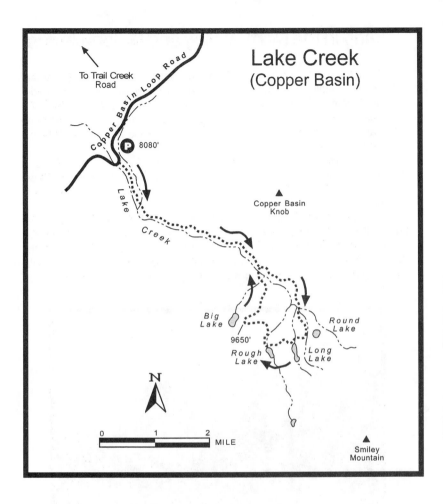

Lake Creek
(Copper Basin)

To Trail Creek Road

Copper Basin Loop Road

P 8080'

Lake Creek

▲ Copper Basin Knob

Big Lake

9650'

Round Lake

Rough Lake

Long Lake

N

0   1   2   MILE

▲ Smiley Mountain

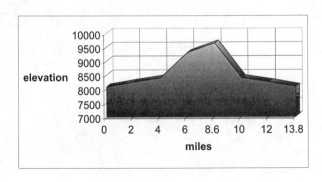

elevation

10000
9500
9000
8500
8000
7500
7000

0   2   4   6   8.6   10   12   13.8

miles

Riding in the North Valley and Galena Areas

When you choose to ride in the Galena Area, you will be blessed with amazing scenery, wildlife, incredible trails, and not many people close to you. One of the gems of this area for riding is Galena Lodge. Between the trails, food, staff, views and ambience, you WILL be blown away. There are some new trails around the area, and what a perfect staging area, a south-facing deck in the mountains!

The Harriman Trail also either ends or begins at Galena Lodge, a rolling gravel and dirt trail which parallels the highway back in the trees. Great location for a family cruise or hardcore's wanting to get their butts worked.

Other North Valley rides, such as Easley Loop and Prairie to Miner Loop will certainly work parts of your body other than your legs. Can you say mental strength?! For a real adventure that's no exaggeration, get on the Baker to Norton ride. You will be amazed at the views, trail finding skills you'll need and incredible, faint trails! Be prepared for anything if you go there.

Crossing over Galena Summit on the old Wagon Road, circa 1914
Courtesy of Community Library, Ketchum, Idaho, Regional History Department

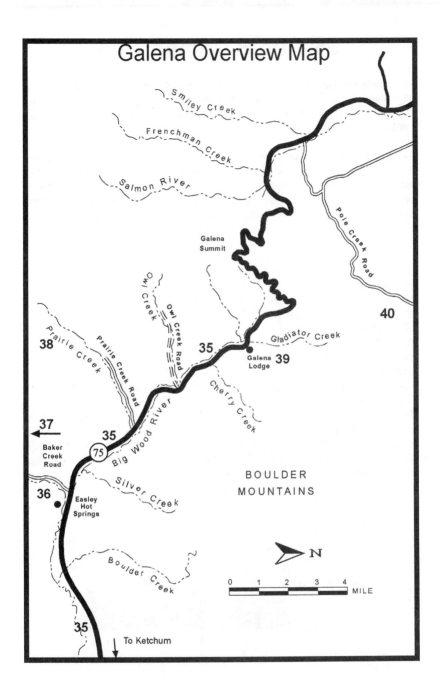

Galena Overview Map

Smiley Creek

Frenchman Creek

Salmon River

Galena Summit

Owl Creek

Owl Creek Road

Prairie Creek

Prairie Creek Road

38

Gladiator Creek

35

Galena Lodge **39**

Cherry Creek

Pole Creek Road

40

37 ←

Baker Creek Road

35 (75)

Big Wood River

36 ●
Easley Hot Springs

Silver Creek

BOULDER MOUNTAINS

Boulder Creek

◣N

0   1   2   3   4 MILE

35

To Ketchum ↓

92

35. The Harriman Trail

The Harriman Trail extends from the SNRA headquarters north of Ketchum all the way up to Galena Lodge. You can either ride up or down the trail, but don't be fooled into thinking it's gradual the entire way. This trail definitely has some ups and some downs.

Getting There: From Ketchum, drive north on Hwy 75 for 7.8 miles and turn right into the parking area for the SNRA headquarters. This is the end point of the ride. For a shuttle, leave a car here and continue driving up Hwy 75 for another 16.2 miles (24 miles total) and turn right into the Galena Lodge parking lot. Of course, you always start anywhere along the trail and go anywhere. Follow the signs, the ride begins here.

Length: 18.6 miles (one-way)
Difficulty Rating: Easy/Moderate
Technical Rating: 1+
The Ride: Start anywhere along the trail and enjoy!
Starting Elevation: 7290'
Ending Elevation: 6280'
Total Elevation Loss: 1010'
Surface: 12' wide pea-gravel trail
Season: May - October
Fun Factor: Beautiful cruise up or down the valley following the Big Wood River and the Boulder Mountains all the way.
Summary: This ride is the perfect introductory ride for the person new to mountain biking or visiting the valley. Because of it's beautifully manicured terrain, you can enjoy this ride and still maintain a conversation. This could be classified as the perfect "first date" ride. No pressure to perform, no tears, good conversation . . .

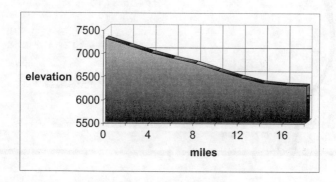

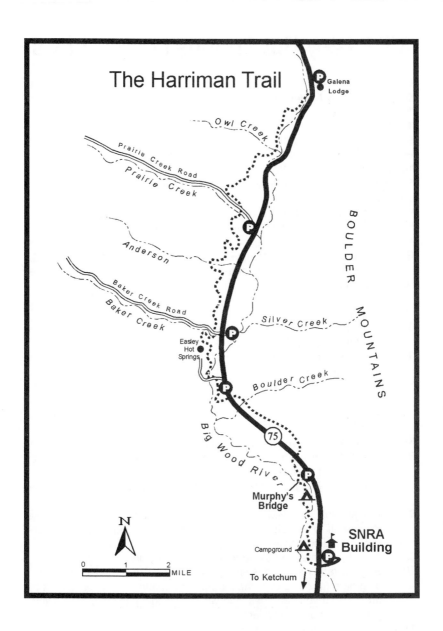

The Harriman Trail

Galena Lodge

Owl Creek

Prairie Creek Road

Prairie Creek

Anderson

Baker Creek Road

Baker Creek

Silver Creek

Easley Hot Springs

Boulder Creek

75

Big Wood River

Murphy's Bridge

SNRA Building

Campground

To Ketchum

N

0   1   2
MILE

BOULDER MOUNTAINS

36. Easley Hot Springs Loop (Curly's)

Length: 12.3 miles
Difficulty Rating: Moderate
Technical Rating: 3 (for the descent)
The Ride: Loop
Starting Elevation: 6675'
High Point Elevation: 8200'
Total Elevation Gain: 1525'
Surface: Dirt jeep road and single track trail
Season: June - October
Fun Factor: Steady moderate climb to an outrageous downhill.
Summary: A gradual climb on a jeep road to a single track downhill that rivals any ride in the area.
Getting There: From Ketchum, drive north on Highway 75 approximately 15.5 miles and park on the right side of the road directly opposite of Baker Creek Road. The ride begins here.

Miles The Ride:

0.0   From the parking area, cross back over the highway and begin riding up Baker Creek Road #162.

3.1   Just after crossing over the East Fork of Baker Creek, turn left onto the East Fork of Baker Creek Road #68 and begin a gradual climb.

5.1   At the fork, take the lower (left), more travelled road which descends for a bit before climbing again.

5.7   Another fork, take the right (upper), more travelled road and begin climbing another pitch.

6.3   Switchbacks, never too hard, but always a good get.

8.0   The saddle with a view and the top of the ride. Although the jeep road keeps going past this point, the top is marked by the end of the switchback and a small turn out on the left of the road next to a small tree. Great views to the west.

8.2   Whoa! While making a right turn on the road, look for the faint jeep trail leading off to the left which quickly becomes a great single-track descent heading down the ridgeline.

8.6   Pass by a watering hole and views of the Boulder Mountains.

10.7 Begin a rather steep descent down the ridgeline. Please avoid skidding here (or going over the bars for that matter), it has become a big problem. If you can't descend without skidding, think about walking your bike through this section.

11.5 The trail comes out next to some cabins, please don't bother the people here. Continue on the dirt roads paralleling the highway until riding onto the highway a couple hundred yards later.

11.7 Turn left onto Highway 75 and ride back to your car.

12.3 The end of the ride and back at the parking area.

Easley Loop

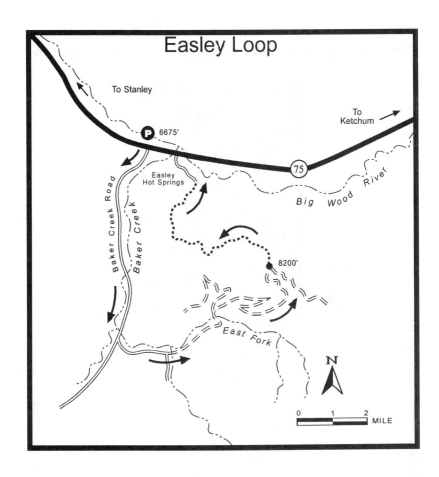

To Stanley

To Ketchum

P 6675'

Easley Hot Springs

75

Big Wood River

Baker Creek Road

Baker Creek

8200'

East Fork

N

0   1   2   MILE

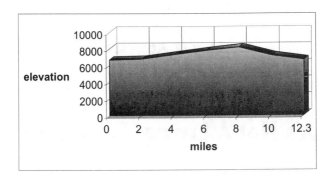

37. Baker Lake to Norton Creek

Length: 12.1 miles
Difficulty Rating: Difficult
Technical Rating: 3+
The Ride: Loop
Starting Elevation: 7300'
High Point Elevation: 9280'
Total Elevation Gain: 1980'
Surface: Dirt jeep road and single track trail
Season: June - October
Fun Factor: Fun? Definitely. Adventurous? You know it.
Summary: This is also known as Apollo Creek Trail. This is a faith ride. Believe and you're in, don't, and you might as well not leave your car. Enjoy!
Getting There: From Ketchum, drive north on Hwy 75 for 15.5 miles and turn left onto Baker Creek Road. Continue on another 6 miles to the junction with Norton & Prairie Lakes Road and park on the right at the junction. The ride begins here. (*This trail may become closed to mountain bikes in the near future, please obey any signs indicating this.)

Miles The Ride:

0.0 Begin by riding up Baker Creek Road heading south and up eventually to the Baker Lake parking area at the end of the road.

3.4 The Baker Lake parking area. Ride across the creek, register yourself and continue up the trail. The trail from here is not too steep...

4.9 Take the right fork leading off to Apollo Creek on trail #139. From here you'll do a traversing descent before grinding and pushing a bit. Here's the faith part of the ride. Follow the cairns and red tape attached to the trees. Pay attention, it's easy to miss them.

5.2 The trail disappears into the meadow. Stay in the dry creek bed, watch -ing for the cairns leading to a tree 150 yards later where the trail reappears and switchbacks a bit before gaining a small saddle.

5.8 First saddle, walk down the scree and begin riding at the edge of the rocks following cairns and red tape for almost a mile.

6.5 Reach the dry creek bed of Apollo Creek. Continue up the other side to the fork in the trail. As the sign indicates, straight ahead is the Baker Lake Trail #138 and the right fork leads down into the Apollo Creek Trail #139. Stay straight traversing along the Baker Lake Trail.

7.3 Gain the saddle leading into the West Fork of Norton Creek drainage. This is where all the fun begins, a great trail and descent.

7.6 Fork in the trail. Turn right into the West Fork of Norton Creek drainage. A left turn here would lead into Bluff and Big Smoky Creeks in the South Fork of the Boise River drainage.

10.7 Junction with Norton Creek, Norton Lakes Trail #135 and the trailhead parking area. Ride across the creek, through the parking area and continue on down the jeep road to your car.

12.1 End of the ride.

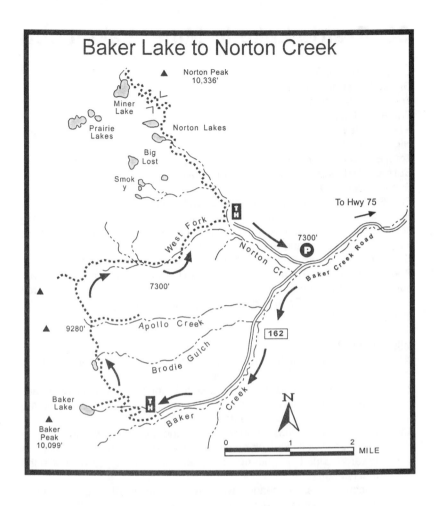

Baker Lake to Norton Creek

Norton Peak
10,336'

Miner Lake

Prairie Lakes

Norton Lakes

Big Lost

Smoky

West Fork

Norton Cr

To Hwy 75

7300'
P

Baker Creek Road

7300'

Apollo Creek

162

9280'

Brodie Gulch

Baker Lake

Baker Creek

Baker Peak
10,099'

N

0   1   2
MILE

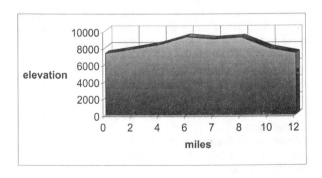

elevation

10000
8000
6000
4000
2000
0

0   2   4   6   7   8   10   12
miles

38. Prairie Lake to Miner Lake Loop

Length: 15.7 miles
Difficulty Rating: Difficult
Technical Rating: 4
The Ride: Loop
Starting Elevation: 6900'
High Point Elevation: 8700'
Total Elevation Gain: 1800'
Surface: Dirt jeep road and single track trail
Season: June - October
Fun Factor: Lakes, creeks, mountains, and swimming.
Summary: Not only is this a great nordic skiing area, but the mountain biking here is phenomenal as well. Technical skills are helpful but not necessary, the grade is gradual and the scenery and swimming is even better!
Getting There: From Ketchum, drive north on Highway 75 for 18.5 miles to Prairie Creek Road. There is a big turn off next to the highway on the left. Park here, this is where the ride begins. (*You could also drive to the parking area at the end of Prairie Creek Road and begin there, saving an additional 2.6 miles.)

Miles The Ride:

0.0 Begin by riding up the Prairie Creek Road which is both gravel, dirt and well traveled in the summertime.

2.6 Reach the trailhead for Prairie Lake and continue on with single track from this point just after crossing the creek. Buckle down and prepare for a continuous but moderate climb.

4.9 After some fun cruising up the valley and some gradual climbing, Minor Lake trail takes off on the left. Stay straight on the main trail up toward Prairie Lake, but make a note, this is where you will rejoin the trail later.

6.8 Encounter a small meadow with the creek running through it. Stay on the right side and cross over the creek at the upper end of the meadow and continue on to the lake.

7.2 Prairie Lake. Great swimming on the eastern side next to the trail. Careful of the creek flowing in, it's freezing! Look for the trail leading to the left and northeast away from the lake area. It should have a sign pointing to Miner Lake. Follow this trail as it mostly contours and climbs (~600') over to Miner Lake.

8.8 Do NOT take the first left at what you will think if the trail leading back down the valley. Go another 25 yards and turn left at the main trail junction.

10.8 Trail junction with the Prairie Lake Trail. Turn right and continue down to the trailhead.

13.1 The Prairie Lake Trailhead. If you parked here, great have a nice drive out, otherwise, continue down the road to your car at Highway 75.

15.7 The end of the ride.

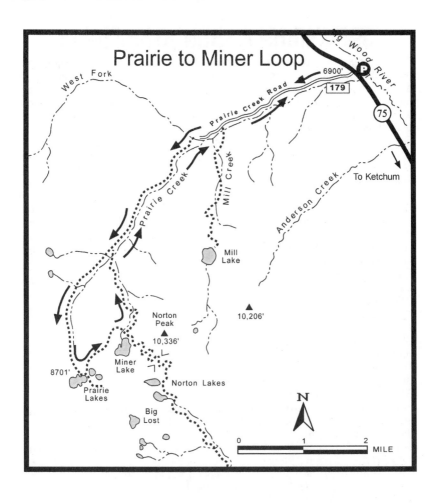

Prairie to Miner Loop

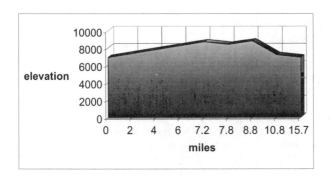

39. Galena Lodge Area Rides

Galena Lodge has been around since 1974 as a cross country skiing and mountain bike/hiking center. Since mountain biking and other outdoor recreation pursuits have increased in popularity over the years, the lodge has taken an aggressive move in creating a great trail network. With old mines and pioneer cabins throughout the area, any ride at Galena Lodge area is a great time. The trails at Galena are all pieces of a puzzle known as the Galena Grinder, a local race utilizing nearly all of the trails there in one form or another. Maps are available for all the trails at the lodge, and the trails are well signed. Go up, have a great time and enjoy a lunch or dinner on the deck in the heart of the Boulder Mountains.

Getting There: From Ketchum, drive north on Hwy 75 for 24 miles until you see the Galena Lodge sign and lodge on the right side of the road. Turn right into the parking lot to begin your fun. If you reach Galena Summit, you've gone too far, but will have an awesome view of the Sawtooth and Boulder Mountains in return.

Galena Trail
Length: 10 miles
Difficulty Rating: Difficult
Technical Rating: 2+
The Ride: Loop
Starting Elevation: 7290'
High Point Elevation: 8200'
Total Elevation Gain: 1090'
Surface: Single-track and jeep road
Season: June - September
Fun Factor: Locals have put many hard hours into making this one of the more classic rides in the upper valley area. Incredible views, climbs and downhills await you!
Summary: Starting with a cruiser up the Senate Meadow, you then climb up the jeep road to a single track trail traversing the mountains all the way down into the gulch by the corrals after passing straight through the gravel pit. From here the trail climbs up and over the hill down into Gladiator Meadow and back to Galena Lodge.

Psycho Trail
Length: 4.8 miles
Difficulty Rating: Difficult
Technical Rating: 2
The Ride: Loop
Starting Elevation: 7290'
High Point Elevation: 7750'
Total Elevation Gain: 460'
Surface: Single-track and jeep road
Season: June - September
Fun Factor: Quick and steep (not too bad). A great warm-up.
Summary: With a nice gradual warm up riding through Gladiator Meadow, you turn left and begin a gradual climb up to the top of Westernhome Gulch. From here you turn left again following the ridgeline, down and up Emma's Gulch and back to Galena Lodge in time for lunch.

Rip & Tear Trail
Length: 4.5 miles
Difficulty Rating: Moderate
Technical Rating: 2
The Ride: Loop
Starting Elevation: 7290'
High Point Elevation: 7800'
Total Elevation Gain: 510'
Surface: Single-track and jeep road
Season: June - September
Fun Factor: Another short, but sweet loop.
Summary: Begin with another gradually climbing warm-up through Gladiator Meadow. At the Forest Service sign showing the Gladiator Pass (straight ahead), you turn right across the creek and begin climbing. As you crest the top of the jeep road, look for the single-track peeling off right on the nordic ski trail. This is where the trail lives up to it's name, eventually taking riders by some yurts before dumping them back to Galena Lodge.

Cherry Creek Loop
Length: 4 miles
Difficulty Rating: Easy
Technical Rating: 2
The Ride: Loop
Starting Elevation: 7290'
High Point Elevation: 7600"
Total Elevation Gain: 310'
Surface: Single-track and jeep road
Season: June - September
Fun Factor: Although mainly a jeep road, this ride will definitely challenge your climbing ability and put you into one of the most beautiful areas around Galena.
Summary: Ride up Senate Meadows on the main road leading right. As the road tops out, a single-track spur descends to the right, eventually making it's way back to the road. Soon after, you will plunge down North Cherry Creek, go left and climb approx. 1000' back to the top of the loop. You can then either go left to the lodge, or go right an connect onto Galena Loop.

Old Toll Road
Length: Approximately 4 miles to the top
Difficulty Rating: Moderate
Technical Rating: 2+
The Ride: Out and Back (or loop with the highway)
Starting Elevation: 7290'
High Point Elevation: 8700'
Total Elevation Gain: 1410'
Surface: Single-track
Season: June - September
Fun Factor: Some of the most amazing views of the entire valley.
Summary: Access from Galena Lodge or the top of Galena Pass. From the lodge, follow the Northwood Trail to the end and go left where it meets the highway. Go left and climb up to the top of the pass.

Half our life is spent trying to find something to do with the time
we have rushed through life trying to save.

— *Will Rogers*

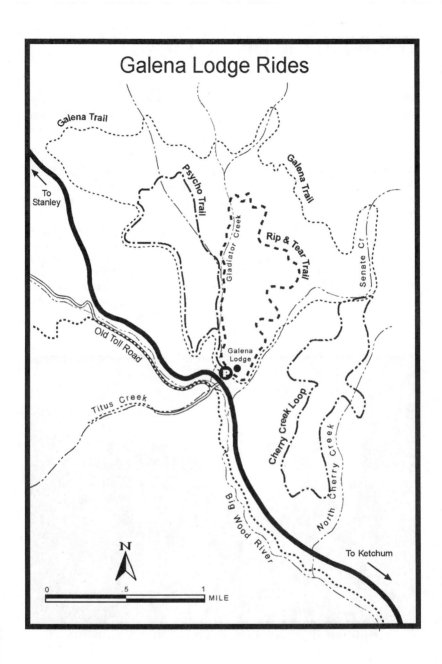

Galena Lodge Rides

Galena Trail

Psycho Trail

Galena Trail

To
Stanley

Gladiator Creek

Rip & Tear Trail

Senate Cr.

Old Toll Road

Galena
Lodge

P

Titus Creek

Cherry Creek Loop

North Cherry Creek

Big Wood River

To Ketchum

N

0   .5   1
MILE

104

Riding in the Stanley Area

When you make the trek up to Stanley, you enter into another world of amazing beauty, abundant wildlife and incredible trails. The Sawtooth Mountains will demand much of your attention as you drive into the area, making you want to stay and play for longer than intended.

Some places not to miss in the area are Redfish Lake Lodge for cocktails lakeside or just a nice refreshing dip in the lake. The Smiley Creek Lodge has a great deck for post ride milkshakes or pre-ride munchies. If you need any outdoor gear in the area, you can visit Riverwear, which carries most all bike parts you could possibly need and then some.

Camping in the Stanley area can get crowded at some of the more popular areas, so feel free to jump into primitive camping mode and hit any dirt road leading off the beaten path. You just won't have a toilet or shower, no biggie.

Basically, get out and have some fun all around the area. There's hiking, biking, swimming, rafting, kayaking, hunting, fishing and picnicing to be had around every corner. Stanley is truely an undiscovered gem of the West. Help us to keep it a special place for everyone to enjoy.

Another typical day in the Sawtooth Mountains
Courtesy of the McBob Collection

There is only one way to achieve happiness on this terrestrial ball,
and that is to have either a clear conscience or none at all.
— *Ogden Nash*

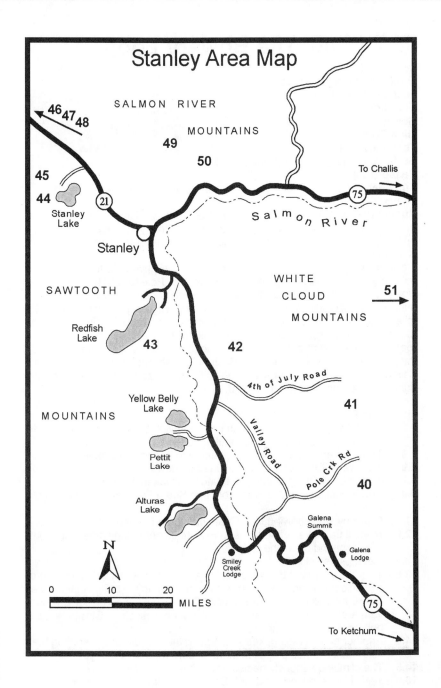

Stanley Area Map

SALMON   RIVER

MOUNTAINS

49

50

46 47 48

45

44

Stanley Lake

21

Stanley

To Challis

75

Salmon River

SAWTOOTH

Redfish Lake

43

42

WHITE

CLOUD

MOUNTAINS

51

4th of July Road

41

Yellow Belly Lake

MOUNTAINS

Pettit Lake

Valley Road

Pole Crk Rd

40

Alturas Lake

Galena Summit

Galena Lodge

N

Smiley Creek Lodge

0   10   20

MILES

75

To Ketchum

40. The Bowery Loop

Length: 30.5 miles
Difficulty Rating: Abusive
Technical Rating: 4
The Ride: Loop
Starting Elevation: 7760'
High Point Elevation: 9060'
Total Elevation Gain: 4670'
Surface: Dirt jeep road and single-track
Season: July - September
Fun Factor: Remote wilderness area with views and serious wildlife...be prepared!

Summary: You'll feel good at the top of Grand Prize Gulch, you'll even feel good by the time you reach Bowery. But by the time you reach the top of the hike-a-bike, you'll be praying to the Endurance Gods for forgiveness. The rest is a classic wilderness ride.

Getting There: From Ketchum, drive north on Highway 75 for just over 37 miles and turn right at the sign pointing the way to "Pole Creek Road and Valley Road." (If you go flying past the Smiley Creek Lodge, you've just gone 0.5 miles too far) If coming from Stanley, go south on Highway 75 for just over 24.5 miles and turn left at the same sign. Stay on the main road heading toward the mountains, passing several spur roads along the way. At 2.3 miles on this road, you cross over Pole Creek and come to a junction. Continue forward on the road heading toward "Germania Basin." The left fork becomes Valley Road. Follow this road for another 4.2 miles to Grand Prize Gulch appears on the right. The ride begins and ends here.

Miles The Ride:

0.0 Begin by finding the trail which crosses over Pole Creek. Just after crossing the creek, be sure to take the left fork 0.3 miles later.

1.5 The road ends at the creek crossing and becomes single-track.

2.9 The switchbacks end in high alpine meadows.

3.7 Just after the main saddle, Gladiator Trail takes off on the right.

9.0 Small junction with the West Fork and South Fork. Stay on the main trail.

11.4 Cross by sign showing Ibex Creek canyon on the right.

12.6 A small trail takes off to the left. Both trails get to the same place, but stay right and cross the creek.

13.4 Gate, please close.

13.6 Take the very faint trail which cuts back to the left just when the guard station comes into view. Follow this trail down to the bridge that crosses over the creek by the guard station. Go through the guard station courtyard area to the gate against the hill on the west side. Close the gate behind you and go right.

14.0 Another gate crossing, keep traversing the hillside before starting the hike-a-bike climbing section in the aspen trees ahead of you.

14.6 The climbing seriously begins now, either push, carry or cry.

16.6 Yes! This is the top, nice job! Scramble up the 9059' peak on the right for killer views of Castle Peak. Careful going down from here, it is seriously loose, steep and dangerous. If you get hurt here, you are a long ways from help!

18.8 The trail intersects Germania Creek, stay left.

19.7 Cross the creek here, anywhere you can and continue riding left and up.

23.2 Junction with Washington Lakes/Chamberlain Lakes Trail. Stay on main trail.

24.7 End of the single-track and junction with Pole Creek Road. Ride up road.

27.8 The top of Pole Creek Summit. It's all downhill from here!

30.5 End of the ride and back at your car.

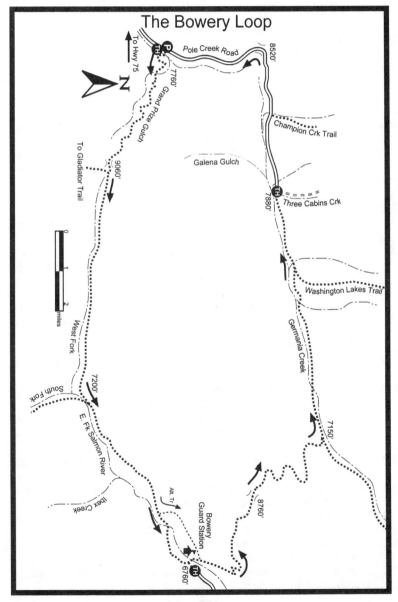

The Bowery Loop

41. Fourth of July to Pole Creek

Length: 38.1 miles
Difficulty Rating: Difficult/Abusive
Technical Rating: 3
The Ride: Loop
Starting Elevation: 6800'
High Point Elevation: 9580'
Total Elevation Gain: 2780'
Surface: Dirt road and single track trail
Season: June - October
Fun Factor: Alpine lakes, great descending and fun climbing.
Summary: Let's say you want one hell of a long ride, some serious uphill with a backcountry commitment that takes the better part of a day. Hey, what a surprise, this is the ride for you. It's gorgeous and you get into areas where not many others go.
Getting There: From Ketchum, drive north 47 miles on Highway 75 over Galena Summit past Smiley Creek Lodge to Fourth of July Creek Road. Turn right here and park anywhere in the sage by the road. This road is approximately 15 miles from Stanley by heading south on Highway 75. The ride begins here.

Miles The Ride:

0.0   Begin by riding up the dirt/gravel road heading east toward the White Cloud Mountains.

1.0   Pass by the Fourth of July Creek Ranch on the right.

1.7   Enter in the trees by the creek. From here, the road winds while climbing gradually through the trees following the creek.

4.1   Cabin ruins and white cliffs on the left.

4.8   Pass by Champion Creek Trailhead on the right.

8.3   A primitive campground on the right marks the beginning of more "aggressive climbing" to come. Gear down.

9.2   A slight break from climbing in the meadows.

10.3 Trailhead. Please register to make the USFS happy. From here, follow the single track trail to the two lakes ahead.

11.8 Trail junction. The left fork leads over the saddle and into Warm Springs Creek eventually joining up with Fisher Creek (very adventurous). In stead, take the right (forward) fork and come to Fourth of July Lake just ahead of you. From here continue on to the lake and up the trail to the saddle with Washington Lake.

12.8 You've reached Washington Lake. Continue on the trail as it descends into Germania Creek.

13.6 At the fork, turn right heading toward Germania Creek where it climbs a short bit before becoming more mellow a half mile later.

15.9 At the fork, turn left and down toward Germania Creek, heading toward the junction of Germania and Washington Creeks.

16.7 Another fork, stay straight (right) and continue riding down a steep section into Germania Creek.

17.6 Trail junction: Join Germania Creek Trail and turn right here climbing slightly up to the main road.

18.9   The Germania Creek Trailhead. Follow the road up and out for the next 3 miles ascending the upper Germania Creek drainage.

22.1   The top of Pole Creek summit.

28.6   Whoa! At the junction, be careful not to miss the right turn here leading up the small hill on Valley Road. Continue on Valley Road all the way to Hwy 75, cruising down the east side of the Salmon River basin.

37.6   End of Valley Road and junction with Hwy 75. Turn right here and continue heading north down Hwy 75 to Fourth of July Creek Road.

38.1   Turn right on Fourth of July Creek Road and return to your car. This is the end of an amazing ride.

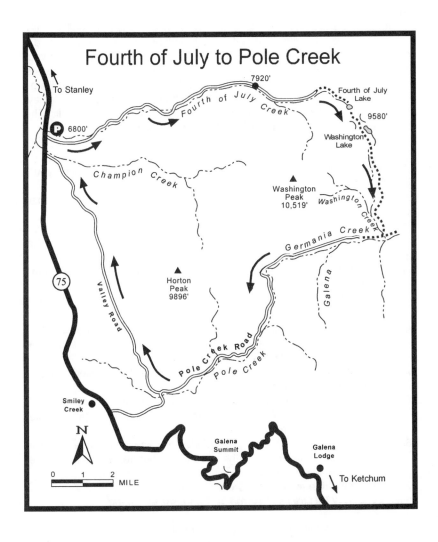

Fourth of July to Pole Creek

42. Fisher Creek

Length: 17.8 miles
Difficulty Rating: Difficult
Technical Rating: 2+
The Ride: Loop
Starting Elevation: 6625'
High Point Elevation: 8125'
Total Elevation Gain: 1500'
Surface: Pavement, dirt jeep road and single track trail
Season: June - October
Fun Factor: The ultimate ride!!
Summary: When you have the time and the want for a ride that you'll be talking about for years to come, this is it. Great climbing, stream crossings and a descent that would make anyone jealous, it's all right here just waiting for you.
Getting There: From Ketchum, drive north on Highway 75 up and over Galena Summit, passing by Smiley Creek Store and Sessions Lodge to the Williams Creek Trailhead at just over 50 miles from Ketchum. If coming from Stanley, drive south on Highway 75 for approximately 13.5 miles to the turn off. The parking area is on the east side of the highway. Park here and gear up.

Miles The Ride:

0.0 Begin by riding up the highway (south) back toward the direction you just came from.

2.3 Turn left onto Fisher Creek Road and begin a gradual cruise up the road for 6.5 miles.

8.4 Begin a very 'rideable' climb which tops out after 1/3 mile. Don't worry if you have to push your bike for a few feet. This is the only place in the ride if you have to.

9.1 You're at the top. Please register yourself so the USFS can keep tabs on the number of riders/hikers per year, and get ready for the ultimate in down hill pleasure. Be sure to take the single-track trail leading west off this saddle.

10.6 Fork in the trail. Take the left fork and continue on the Fisher Creek Loop which gradually winds and climbs its way up the small valley. The right fork leads to Warm Springs Meadow.

12.7 Another saddle. From here be careful and enjoy the bobsled descent for the next 3+ miles.

16.0 Cross over the bridge/creek and into a pristine meadow for a little re grouping. Continue left and up toward a small switchback (all rideable) and begin a fairly small climb.

16.4 Top of the last climb and only descending lies ahead. Be sure to take in the view of the Sawtooths in the last clearing before the end of the ride. You'll know where I mean.

17.8 End of the ride at Williams Creek Trailhead.

(This trail sponsored by Team Smiley Creek)

"What irritates us most about others is
most often what we dislike about ourselves."

Fisher Creek

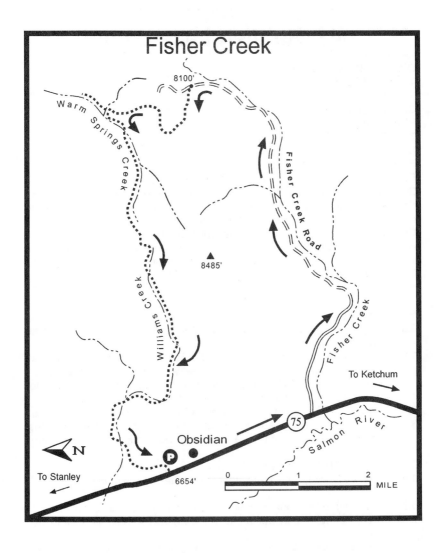

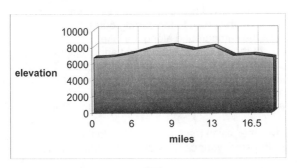

112

43. Redfish Lake Loop

Length: 13.9 miles
Difficulty Rating: Difficult
Technical Rating: 3
The Ride: Loop
Starting Elevation: 6550'
High Point Elevation: 7560'
Total Elevation Gain: 1940'
Surface: Single track trail and pavement
Season: Mid June - October
Fun Factor: Beautiful views of White Cloud Mountains, wildlife and the lake!
Summary: The loop around Redfish may seem like a little afternoon jaunt, but don't let the map fool you. This is a difficult, technical ride that'll make you beg the campers at the far end of the lake for food.
Getting There: From Ketchum drive North on Hwy 75 to the Redfish Lake Road turn-off (approx. 55 miles). From Stanley, drive south on Highway 75 for just over 4 miles. At 2 miles down the road pass the Redfish Lodge sign and junction on the right. Just past this junction on the main road is a parking area on the right. Park/start here.

Miles The Ride:

0.0 Begin by riding out of the parking area heading south on the paved road toward Sockeye Campground.

1.6 After passing by Sandy Beach and Mt. Heyburn Campground, turn into Sock eye Campground and go left (the wrong way) onto the one-way road. Turn left onto the single track trail #045 with the sign pointing to "Decker Flats", and pass behind the campground bathrooms.

2.1 Begin a gradual roller-coaster climb with some steeps here and there.

3.1 Gain the summit ridge and check out the beautiful views of the Sawtooths, Stanley basin and Redfish Lake. Please watch for horses in this section.

3.3 Sign for Elk Meadow turns left, stay straight on the main trail.

4.0 Sign for Decker Flats trail #400 on left. Stay on main trail along the ridge.

5.9 At the signed junction, turn right and down towards the lake.

7.8 A very techy section, be careful of the wet rocks and logs close to the lake.

8.0 Junction: stay right on main trail or hike on the left trail to some falls.

8.2 In a tree'd and washy area look for the bridge crossing the creek and follow that trail around and behind the Inlet Campground. Follow this trail along the fence next to the campground, then you will start to ride away from the campground along the lake.

9.4 Junction: At the switchback, stay right and continue climbing up.

10.6 Just past the top of the climbing is a trail junction. The left trail leads to Bench Lakes. Stay along the ridge on the main trail heading down.

13.5 Junction: Stay right and down along Fishhook Creek. Shortly afterward, a small trail leads to the left to the Redfish Corrals, don't go there either.

13.8 Cross over the paved road and continue to the parking area.

13.9 The parking area, your car and the end of another epic, fun ride!

Redfish Lake Loop

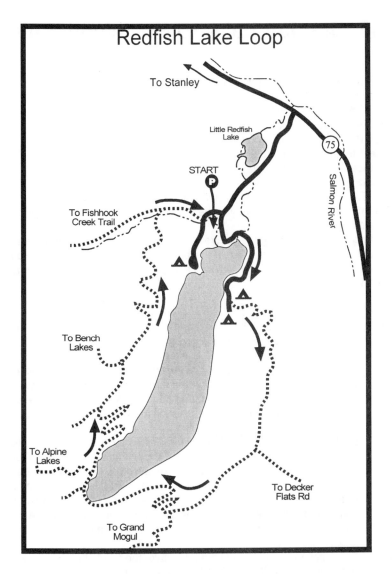

To Stanley

Little Redfish Lake

75

Salmon River

START
P

To Fishhook
Creek Trail

To Bench
Lakes

To Alpine
Lakes

To Grand
Mogul

To Decker
Flats Rd

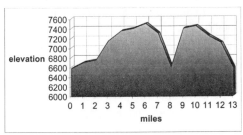

elevation

7600
7400
7200
7000
6800
6600
6400
6200
6000

0 1 2 3 4 5 6 7 8 9 10 11 12 13
miles

114

44. Stanley Lake to Bridalveil Falls

Length: 14.2 miles
Difficulty Rating: Easy/Moderate
Technical Rating: 2
The Ride: Out and back
Starting Elevation: 6350'
High Point Elevation: 7400'
Total Elevation Gain: 1050'
Surface: Gravel road, single track trail
Season: June - September
Fun Factor: Gorgeous views of the Sawtooth Mountains.
Summary: This ride can give you the views, waterfalls, the Sawtooth Mountains and a lake to swim in.
Getting There: From Stanley, drive west on Highway 21 for five miles and park on the left side of the road at the beginning of the Stanley Lake Road. This is where the ride begins. You can also just drive up the road to the lake and forget potential traffic.

Miles The Ride:

0.0 Begin by riding along the main road heading west toward Stanely Lake. Climb slowly through the forest and be sure to stay on the main road to the lake.

3.5 Go left on the road heading toward the boat launch and pass by the Inlet Campground. Ride to the end of the turnaround and turn right toward the Alpine Way Trailhead. From here the trail is a nice raised gravelly trail trail over water-logged areas. Great for strollers, bike trailers, etc., until the dirt
climbing ahead, which is where the trail picks up in steepness and fun!

4.8 The Alpine Way Trail goes off to the left and enters the Sawtooth Wilderness Area. The SWA is off-limits to mountain bikes, but a great place for a hike on another day. Continue on and stay straight on the main trail. After this the trail levels out a bit and roller-coasters through the forest. You'll eventually see two trails (one after the other) lead off to the right going to the falls. Take a picture, be careful and watch out for slippery rocks!

7.1 Trail junction and the top of the ride. Take the trail to the right to go check out Bridalveil Falls. The left fork enters the Sawtooth Wilderness Area again. Turn around here and enjoy the ride back down to your car.

14.2 The end of the ride.

A day without laughter is a day wasted.
— *Charlie Chaplin*

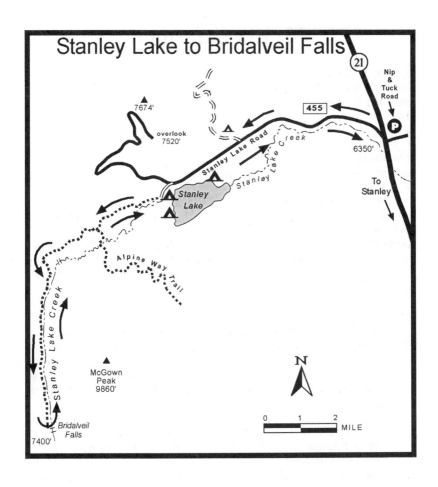

Stanley Lake to Bridalveil Falls

21

Nip
&
Tuck
Road

455

P

7674'

overlook
7520'

Stanley Lake Road

Stanley Lake Creek

6350'

To
Stanley

Stanley
Lake

Stanley Lake Creek

Alpine Way Trail

N

Stanley Lake Creek

McGown
Peak
9860'

Bridalveil
Falls
7400'

0   1   2
MILE

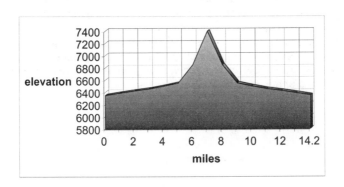

elevation

7400
7200
7000
6800
6600
6400
6200
6000
5800

0   2   4   6   8   10   12   14.2

miles

45. Elk Mountain

Length: 12.4 miles
Difficulty Rating: Moderate
Technical Rating: 2
The Ride: Loop
Starting Elevation: 6550'
High Point Elevation: 7000'
Total Elevation Gain: 450'
Surface: Dirt jeep road and single track trail
Season: June - October
Fun Factor: Wildlife, wildflowers, rocks, roots and mountains.
Summary: With gorgeous views and plenty of wildlife, you get Elk Mountain loop. Bring bug juice, food and a camera.
Getting There: From Stanley, drive west on Highway 21 for five miles and turn left on Stanley Lake Road #455. Drive just over 3.5 miles (passing by the Inlet C.G.) to the Elk Mountain Road #649 and park in the day-use area. The ride begins here.

Miles The Ride:

0.0 Begin by riding up Elk Mountain road, which is a gradual grind up.

1.8 Whoa! Look left for the Elk Meadow Loop trailhead and turn left here. If you want a real grind, continue up the main road to the top for a great view after another 1.3 miles and 600 feet. The trail from here becomes rather technical going over rocks and tree roots all the while descending.

3.5 Whoa! Welcome to Elk Meadows. Be careful not to continue into the meadow and get inundated with skeeters, elk and mud. Instead, take the faint trail to the right while staying on the right or east side of the meadow.

5.2 Turn right on the trail paralleling Elk Creek, which ascends gradually through the trees.

6.5 Continue forward and down, slowly contouring the mountain. Hold on, this is some fun, fast downhill cruising! There are a few signs on the trail from here to keep you going the right way.

9.8 Trail junction: go right and shortly thereafter, up the small hill.

11.2 After cruising through a camping area, join Stanley Lake Road. Go right and follow the road back to your car at the day-use area.

12.4 The end of the ride and back at your car.

"Nature makes no mistakes."

Elk Mountain

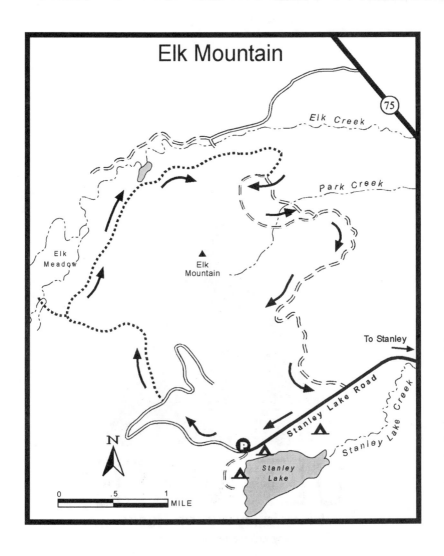

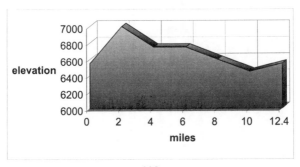

Bicycle Hydration Packs

www.ultimatedirection.com

46. Valley Creek-Knapp Creek Loop

Length: 21.1 miles
Difficulty Rating: Easy/Moderate
Technical Rating: 1+
The Ride: Loop
Starting Elevation: 6647'
High Point Elevation: 7290'
Total Elevation Gain: 643'
Surface: Dirt jeep road and single-track trail
Season: June - October
Fun Factor: Elk, beautiful meadows, killer trail and the mountains.
Summary: This is a ride you will remember at least 'til the next one. Actually, this is a modified ATV trail that kicks some serious mountain biking butt! It is mellow and fun!
Getting There: From Stanley, drive west on Highway 21 for 11.1 miles and turn right on Rd #203. At 11.9 miles you'll pass the Blind Summit sign, and at 14.3 miles, turn right and park close to the sign pointing to Valley Creek trailhead. The ride starts here.

Miles The Ride:

0.0 Begin by continuing up the road toward the Valley Creek trailhead.

0.9 At the obvious junction, stay to the left.

1.6 Another junction, stay to the right here.

2.4 Yet another junction, stay right here too.

3.1 Ah, finally, the Valley Creek trailhead. Seriously, it gets incredible from here!

7.3 Here you encounter a small climb.

7.8 Prospect Creek is on the right. Stay straight.

8.6 Major Junction: Go left toward Cape Horn Guard Station and Knapp Creek.

9.2 Big creek crossing over Knapp Creek, followed by another major junction. Take a left here toward the Cape Horn Guard Station.

11.4 Stay left at the junction and continue following Knapp Creek down. The trail leading off to the right goes to Winnemucca Creek.

14.5 The Knapp Creek trailhead. Follow the gravel-dirt road down to Cape Horn.

18.6 At USFS #203 (the first main road), stay left and start looking for elk grazing in the evenings and mornings.

19.3 Pass by the Cape Horn Guard Station on the left.

21.1 Hey look! Is that your car? If so, the ride is over. If not, you're lost and refer to the map for more information. Now pay attention next time, huh?

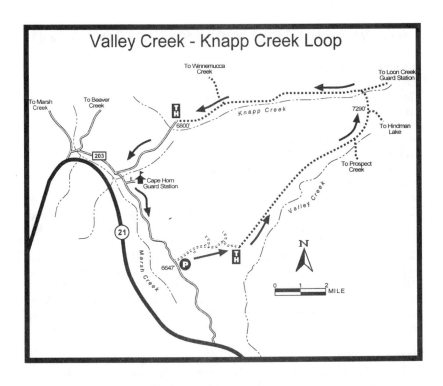

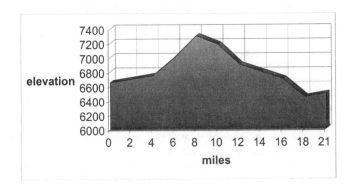

47. Winnemucca Creek-Beaver Creek Loop

Length: 13.4 miles
Difficulty Rating: Moderate
Technical Rating: 2+
The Ride: Loop
Starting Elevation: 6850'
High Point Elevation: 7900'
Total Elevation Gain: 1050'
Surface: Dirt jeep road and single-track trail
Season: June - October
Fun Factor: Elk, beautiful meadows, killer trail and the mountains.
Summary: This is a another ride you will remember at least 'til the next one. This is another modified ATV trail that is seriously fun! Aside from the few climbs it is fairly mellow and extremely gorgeous.
Getting There: From Stanley, drive west on Highway 21 for 18 miles and turn right into the Seafoam Area. As the road forks, stay right again immediately. At 18.5 miles, bear left toward Beaver Creek Campground. Then at 23.8 miles turn right toward Loon Creek Guard Station. And at 26.7 miles from Stanley and 8.3 miles from Highway 21, park on the right in the primitive camping area on the right just before crossing over Beaver Creek. The ride begins here.

Miles The Ride:

0.0 Begin by continuing up the main road you just came in on and over Beaver Creek. After a little climb and 0.1 miles, turn right toward Winnemucca Creek.

0.8 Trail junction: The right fork leads over to Knapp Creek, but instead continue on the main trail heading up Winnemucca Creek.

5.5 The trail begins to gradually climb a bit from here.

6.0 A short, steep climb enters the picture followed by more gradual climbing.

6.5 Ah, the top of the climbing portion of the ride. It's all downhill from here!

7.2 At the short marshy area, please be cautious of eroding the trail any more than it already is. After this, you encounter a short, steep hill followed immediately by a crossing of Beaver Creek.

7.8 Trail junction: Stay left here and continue down the trail descending Beaver Creek.

9.5 Trail junction with Beaver Creek Trail, stay left and continue down.

9.8 The single-track trail ends at Beaver Creek Road. Stay left here and cruise down the road toward your car.

13.4 The end of the ride and back at your car. Hope you had as much fun as we did.

"The wise person listens more than he speaks."

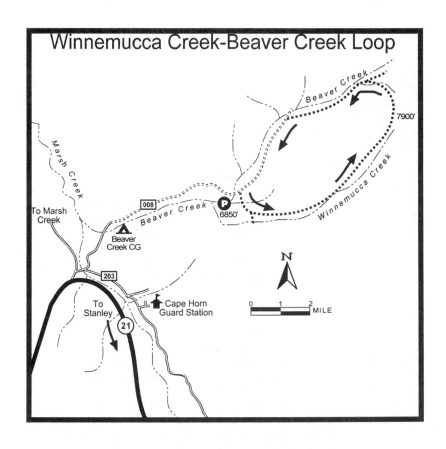

Winnemucca Creek-Beaver Creek Loop

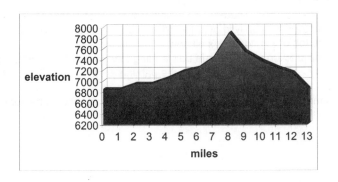

48. Wyoming Creek

Length: 25.6 miles
Difficulty Rating: Difficult
Technical Rating: 3+
The Ride: Loop
Starting Elevation: 6980'
High Point Elevation: 8400'
Total Elevation Gain: 2360'
Surface: Dirt jeep road and single-track trail
Season: Mid-June - October
Fun Factor: You will be in an area that most people only dream of seeing.
Summary: You go from pavement to jeep road and then to single track working you from the start to the finish. You will be tired, thirsty and hungry for more. This is an amazing adventure ride!
Getting There: From Stanley, drive west on Highway 21 for 24.2 miles and park on the right in the pull-out just past the turn to Bull Trout Lake. The ride begins here.

Miles The Ride:

0.0 Begin by riding back down Hwy 21 for 2.8 miles and turn left onto Bound ary Creek Road and ride to the summit.

5.9 The top of Boundary Creek Road. Go down and stay on the main road.

8.3 Fir Creek Trail takes off to the left, stay on the road. This trail actually intersects Wyoming Creek Trail near it's summit.

11.4 Enter into Bruce Meadows and go by the landing strip shortly.

12.5 Rest area. Stay on the main road heading south toward Wyoming Creek.

13.6 Turn left on Wyoming Creek Road, just after a left side spur road.

14.4 The official Wyoming Creek Trailhead. Follow the single track trail.

18.8 Junction with Fir Creek Trail on the left. Continue up Wyoming Creek Trail.

19.0 The top of the climbing and 8400'.

20.5 Enter into the burned-out matchstick forest. Watch for sandy soil.

22.0 The trail goes up and over the ridge in a sort of hike-a-bike...it's quick!

22.6 The top of the ridge. It's all downhill from here!

24.7 Trail junction with the main trail leading toward Bull Trout Lake area. Stay on the main trail and into the parking area. Then follow that road back out to Highway 21.

27.7 Junction with Highway 21, turn right and your car should be right there on the shoulder. This is the end of the ride.

Wyoming Creek

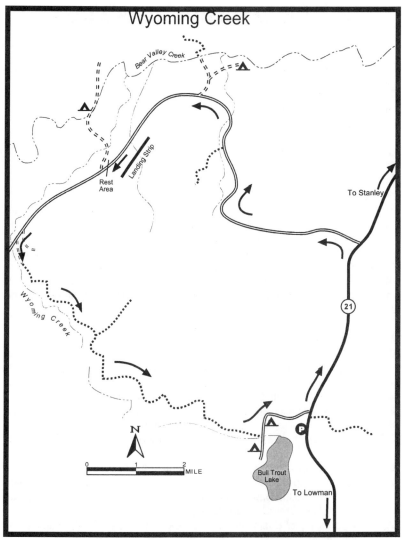

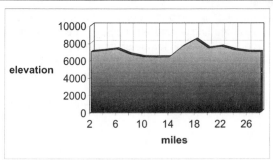

49. Little Basin Creek Loop

Length: 14.3 miles
Difficulty Rating: Moderate
Technical Rating: 2+
The Ride: Loop
Starting Elevation: 6600'
High Point Elevation: 7450'
Total Elevation Gain: 1250'
Surface: Dirt jeep road and single-track
Season: June - October
Fun Factor: The feeling of being in the middle of nowhere, but you're not...really.
Summary: This is destined to be another Fisher Creek ride someday. Get there before the crowds do. Amazing downhills, fun climbs and if you bonk the wolves will take care of you. Just kidding.
Getting There: From Stanley, drive west on Highway 21 for five miles to Stanley Creek Road, turn right and go 1.4 miles to a big brown map board and go left. At the next junction, just over the creek, go right and follow this road for 2.9 miles (total mileage from Highway 21 is 4.3 miles. Park on the right in the clearing, the ride begins here.

Miles The Ride:

0.0 Begin by riding up road #653. At the mining ruins at 0.4 miles, stay to the right and against the hillside on the double-track jeep trail.

1.0 Cross over Stanley Creek and the fun really begins.

2.0 The climbing begins and eases off a short distance later.

2.5 Top of the climbing and the downhill begins into Little Basin Creek...yehaa!

2.8 Enter into a gigantic meadow. Careful of the elk!

3.6 Junction with Little Basin Creek. Follow the single-track downhill from here.

5.6 After the luge-style downhill, be careful of the boulder field.

7.0 Major Junction: After crossing over Basin Creek, go right at the junction and descend the Basin Creek trail. If you were to go left, you would be on the "Hay Creek - Knapp Creek Trail".

7.4 Big crossing of Basin Creek. We looked, there is NO alternative to getting wet.

8.1 Take the switchbacks up and around the muddy bog. It's a quick climb.

9.1 Pass by a trail leading up and left into Hay Creek. Stay on the main trail.

10.6 In the large meadow, look for the sign pointing to Kelly Creek. Cross Basin Creek here and begin a casual ride up Kelly Creek.

12.3 At the junction with the jeep road, go right and continue the casual climbing.

14.3 After a quick little descent, you're back at your car and the ride is over.

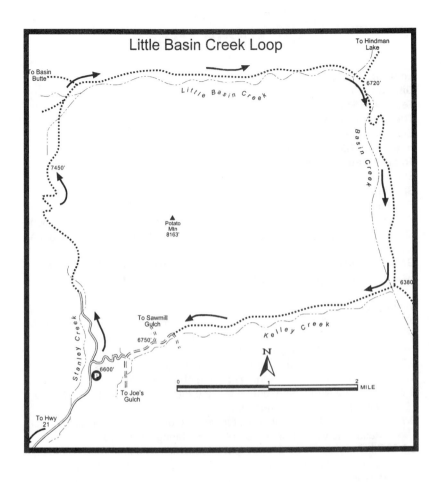

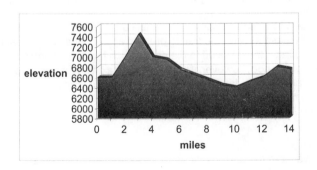

50. Basin Creek

Length: 11.4 miles
Difficulty Rating: Easy
Technical Rating: 1+
The Ride: Out and back
Starting Elevation: 6050'
High Point Elevation: 6650'
Total Elevation Gain: 600'
Surface: Dirt jeep road and single track trails
Season: June - October
Fun Factor: Cruiser, whitewater, wild flowers, and wildlife.
Summary: Yet another sleepy little ride tucked away in the mountains around Stanley. This ride is a blast, roller-coasting your way up the valley on a jeep road and then to a single track trail.
Getting There: From Stanley, drive north on Highway 75 for 8.2 miles to the Basin Creek Campground and park on the left. The ride begins here.

Miles The Ride:

0.0 Begin by riding up and next to the campground on the main dirt road on the north side of Basin Creek. There is a hot spring in the creek here for some good soaking after the ride.

0.7 Spur road on the right, stay on the main road at all times.

1.1 A corral on the right is the beginning of a short climb.

2.2 After crossing over a foot bridge, the road forks. Take the left fork following Basin Creek drainage.

2.7 End of the dirt road in a big turn around area. Follow the single track trail up the valley from here, roller-coastering as you go.

3.8 After crossing over a small foot bridge, there is a spur road on the right and Noho Creek on the left. Stay on the main trail heading up Basin Creek.

4.2 Kelly Creek is on the left. There is a nice single-track trail ascending up the Kelly Creek drainage, but stay on the main trail heading up Basin Creek.

4.6 Enter into a huge meadow with a shale bridge. Pass through the meadow and please stay on the trail to prevent any unnecessary impact.

5.7 Hay Creek trail exits off to the right, which fades out shortly. This is the top of this ride, however, if you want to be a bit adventurous, continue on up the valley as far as you can go. Otherwise, turn around, head down and have some fun!

11.4 End of the ride and back at the campground.

"Until we learn the lessons inherent in unpleasant experiences, they will continue to hold power over us, and we will feel compelled to repeat them."

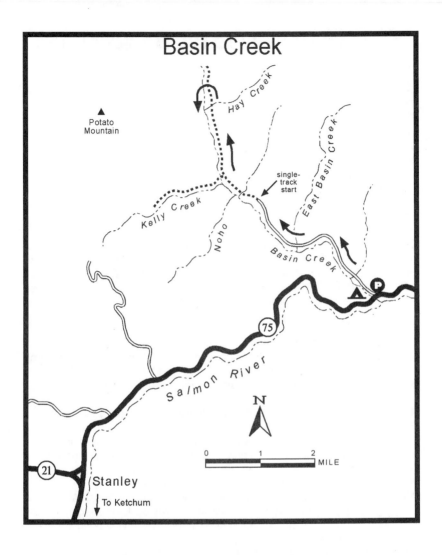

Basin Creek

Potato Mountain

Hay Creek

Kelly Creek

Noho

East Basin Creek

single-track start

Basin Creek

75

Salmon River

N

0   1   2   MILE

21

Stanley

To Ketchum

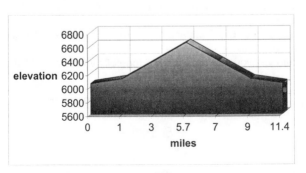

elevation

6800
6600
6400
6200
6000
5800
5600

0   1   3   5.7   7   9   11.4

miles

128

51. Little Boulder to Big Boulder Loop

Length: 24.7 miles
Difficulty Rating: Difficult
Technical Rating: 4
The Ride: Loop
Starting Elevation: 6100'
High Point Elevation: 9600'
Total Elevation Gain: 4600'
Surface: Dirt jeep road and single track trails
Season: June - October
Fun Factor: Wild place with wildlife, wild flowers and wildly amazing views!
Summary: You will get worked, so prepare accordingly. From desert like scapes to high alpine meadows and lakes. The downhill will freak you out it's SO good!
Getting There: From Stanley, drive north on Highway 75 to the East Fork of the Salmon River Road and turn right (30 minute drive). Drive 18 miles to the turn off for Livingston Mine and park immediately on the right at that junction next to the creek. The ride begins here. **You can also do this ride in reverse for a boulder-hopping downhill not to be forgotten.

<u>**Miles**</u> <u>**The Ride:**</u>
0.0 Begin by riding up the main road heading up the East Fork (main rd).
2.8 Little Boulder Creek trailhead parking area. Ride past it on the road and turn right onto the trail about 400 yards past the parking area.
3.5 After blowing a lung at the start, the trail mellows slightly in the main cnyn.
4.8 The sign-in box. Please, please, please sign your party in!
9.4 Trail junction: turn right toward Frog Lake and Boulder Chain Lakes.
11.4 Trail junction: turn right toward Frog Lake and pay no attention to the USFS sign which says it's only 1.25 miles back to the last junction...it's wrong.
11.8 Welcome to Frog Lake. Watch out for the Bovine's.
13.8 The top of the climbing with amazing views in all directions! Wow! Now get ready for an amazing downhill all the way back to your car. Please watch out for hikers and backpackers, as this is a very popular route you're descending.
16.9 Pass by the turn off to Little Redfish Lake on the right.
18.0 Trail junction: somehow the USFS got this mileage wrong, too. Continue down the trail.
20.3 The trailhead for Big Boulder Creek. Should be lots of cars and people on the weekends.
24.7 The road junction with East Fork. Hopefully your car is still there...

It's much easier to turn a friendship into love,
than love into friendship.
— Proverb

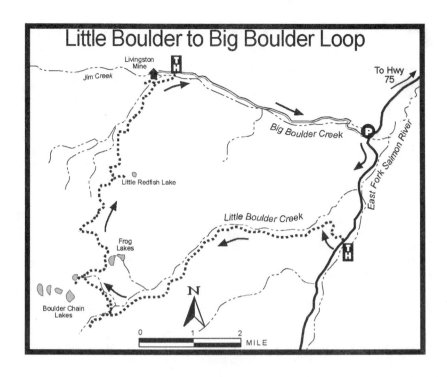

Little Boulder to Big Boulder Loop

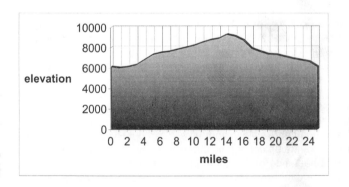

Appendix A: Multi-Day & Adventurous Rides

1. Norton Creek to Big Smoky - Starting in the Baker Creek drainage north of Ketchum, ride up and over Norton Creek into the Big Smoky drainage, eventually coming out at the Skillern Hot Springs and Big Smoky Campground, close to Featherville in the South Fork of the Boise River drainage.

2. North Fork Big Lost River to Bowery Hot Springs - Near the end of the North Fork of the Big Lost River Road, head north to Hunter Creek Summit. From here you'll descend into East Pass Creek and then to Bowery Creek. From the East Fork of the Salmon River Road, turn left and ride up to the hot springs.

3. Alturas Lake to Atlanta - From Alturas Lake on the southern end of the Sawtooth Mountains, ride up and over into the Ross Fork Basin toward Ross Fork Lakes. Turn NW into Decker Creek drainage and follow this into Atlanta. (There are other variations to this adventure, check with the USFS for trail improvements, etc.)

4. Little Casino to Big Casino Loop - This trail will be getting some improvements in the coming years, so put it on your to-do list for the near future.

5. Boundary to Williams Creek - From Highway 75 near the Sawtooth Fish Hatchery, follow Boundary Creek up and over the ridgeline heading east and eventually coming out near The Meadows in Warm Springs Creek. You can either ride out north to the Salmon River or south to finish up on Fisher Creek.

6. Lick Creek - Just over Dollarhide Summit out Warm Springs Creek you'll find a one-way trail called Lick Creek. The USFS will be doing improvements on this trail in the near future.

7. Middle Fork to South Fork of Warm Springs - This has been a heinous linkage in the past, but now the USFS is creating huge trail improvements (summer 2001). The resulting ride will be a loop topping out on the ridge looking down into the Willow Creek drainage before looping around to Poison Flats and back to the start.

8. Johnstone Creek to Pioneer Cabin Loop - This is not very popular due to the trail not being very well suited for mountain bikes. Keep this in mind when you're pushing and walking your bike. Start out Hyndman Creek up East Fork Canyon and ride up Johnstone Creek to Pioneer Cabin. From there ride/walk down the east side of the cabin into the North Fork of Hyndman Creek and back to your car. Save this for when you've done everything else.

9. Hailey to Copper Basin Loop - From Hailey, ride out Quigley Canyon, up and over into the Little Wood River drainage. Turn up Porcupine Creek and into the headwaters of the Little Wood River. Drop down to the Copper Creek Trail and into Copper Basin. How you get back is up to you.

10. Hindman Lake - From Basin Creek Campground on the Salmon River, ride up the creek to Hindman Lake. From there you can either ride back down the same way, or take the trail to Basin Butte, eventually coming down by Nip & Tuck outside Stanley. This would be a very long one-day ride. Always have a back-up plan.

11. Couch Summit to Big Smoky - From the top of Couch Summit by the Soldier Mountains, follow the jeep road across the ridges before dropping down into Miller Creek just outside of the Big Smoky Campground.

12. The Warm Springs Trail - From Bull Trout Lake outside Stanley on Highway 20, follow Dead Man Creek (Warm Springs Trail) all the way down to Bonneville Hot Springs. Don't be fooled into thinking this is an easy downhill ride, or you'll really get worked!

The Authors Story (embellished version)

This is the part where we get to spew something ridiculous about ourselves to you, our captive audience, who is either driving to a trailhead right now and you just happened upon this page, or else you're sitting on the toilet. Don't read too long there, you'll get roids!

So Here We Go...

Greg and Darla McBob (family nickname) are both born and raised Idahoans. They have been enjoying the Wood River and Sawtooth Valleys since they were born and continue to actively pursue their dreams locally. (Those dreams would also include things like trailside yoga, peak-meditation, margarita-chanting at sundown and climbing the walls of the house, as you'll never really know what we mean there...)

As a little girl, Darla used to be bathed in the local hot springs around Stanley by her parents, who built many of the roads around central Idaho. Now today, she bathes occasionally, but still enjoys the hot springs. Greg, on the other hand, grew up mostly in Pocatello (the other windy city), but spent every waking moment he could at the old family cabin out Eagle Creek north of Ketchum. (The fact that it's still standing amazes everyone who has ever partied there)

Greg and Darla met in Ketchum, became best friends, got married, and are currently raising their little girl, Quinn. (Or maybe it's the other way around, we're still not sure. If you have kids, you know what we're talking about)

Today the McBobs enjoy composing symphonic music, writing plays, singing opera, defending stupid-assed lawsuits and creating new rhythm dances with the neighborhood dogs. Darla is pursuing a business in Interior Re-design with a flair for creating unique wall colorations unable to be repeated. Greg, on the other hand, is currently getting his doctorate in Sales Rep Stress Management, with an emphasis in Humanis Hangis Fromwallis, a relatively new field in business play management.

The McBobbies (as they are called in New Zealand) started writing this guidebook originally back in 1995, and after three years of research on all of the trails they compiled their information and created the first Good Dirt in 1998. They wrote the original Good Dirt in response to getting pissed off at the other guidebooks in the area that were on the market for inaccurate information. Sad, but true. The first ride documented was Fox Peak. There is no last ride documented, as we're always out there riding new trails and redocumenting existing trails for changes, reroutes, etc.

If you're a guidebook author, you understand that this is a passion writing a guidebook with the only reward being personal and not financial. Please enjoy this book, and love it as much as the McBob's have in creating it.